The Psychology
of Relationships

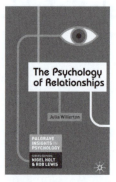
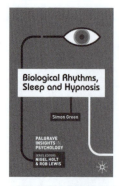
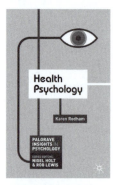

The Psychology of Relationships

Julia Willerton

PALGRAVE
INSIGHTS IN
PSYCHOLOGY

SERIES EDITORS:
NIGEL HOLT
& ROB LEWIS

palgrave
macmillan

First published 2010 by
PALGRAVE MACMILLAN

Palgrave Macmillan in the UK is an imprint of Macmillan Publishers Limited, registered in England, company number 785998, of Houndmills, Basingstoke, Hampshire RG21 6XS.

Palgrave Macmillan in the US is a division of St Martin's Press LLC, 175 Fifth Avenue, New York, NY 10010.

Palgrave Macmillan is the global academic imprint of the above companies and has companies and representatives throughout the world.

Palgrave® and Macmillan® are registered trademarks in the United States, the United Kingdom, Europe and other countries.

ISBN: 978–0–230–24941–7

This book is printed on paper suitable for recycling and made from fully managed and sustained forest sources. Logging, pulping and manufacturing processes are expected to conform to the environmental regulations of the country of origin.

A catalogue record for this book is available from the British Library.

A catalog record for this book is available from the Library of Congress.

10 9 8 7 6 5 4 3 2 1
19 18 17 16 15 14 13 12 11 10

Printed and bound in Great Britain by
CPI Antony Rowe, Chippenham and Eastbourne

Contents

List of figures and tables		vi
Note from series editors		vii
1	Studying relationships: perspectives and methods	1
2	An evolutionary perspective on human relationships	19
3	The effects of early experience on relationships	40
4	Getting relationships started	60
5	Regulating relationships	81
6	Breakdown of relationships	100
7	Cultural variations in relationships	121
8	Effects of relationships	143
	Glossary	162
	References	169
	Index	191
	Reading guide	195

List of figures and tables

Figures

3.1 Adult attachment types   50
6.1 Divorces, rate per thousand, 1971 to 2006   105
7.1 Love scores in love marriages and arranged marriages   137
7.2 Liking in love marriages and arranged marriages   138
8.1 Suicide rates of American men per hundred thousand people   149
8.2 Suicide rates of American women per hundred thousand   149

Tables

3.1 The strange situation   45
3.2 The Love Quiz   48
5.1 Dealing with conflict   92
6.1 Reasons for ending a short-term relationship   103
7.1 Relationships in 37 countries   126
8.1 Rates of depression per 100,000   148
8.2 Social support index and mortality   158

Note from series editors

There are some areas of psychology that really are universal. Most of us are either in relationships, have been in them or like to be in them. We all have experience of how our behaviour and the behaviour of others influence our relationships. This area of psychology is of huge interest to many people whether studying the topic academically or reading for self-improvement or interest.

Julia Willerton is closely involved in teaching and examining students both at pre-university level and as undergraduates. This book adds to her growing list of publications and will form an important addition to this series. Julia was approached to write this book because of her knowledge of presenting material in such a way that it appeals to different levels of study and an ability to explain often difficult-to-grasp theories in ways that will engage lecturers, and students at many different levels. She has taken great care with the organization of this book and has read widely to produce a relationships text that is not merely the usual, well-known material with which many of you may be familiar. It includes the old favourites but extends them and brings them right up to date.

- *You may be reading this book in preparation for your university study.* If this is the case, you will find there are many degrees where the study of relationships is relevant and should be confident in the material delivered by Willerton here. This book is a strong introductory text that will develop your thinking, and extend significantly the coverage provided by general introductory texts in, for instance, psychology, counselling or sociology where it will find a natural home.

- *You may be reading this book while at university.* It may form part of your recommended reading, or you may be extending yourself or preparing for some coursework. The material is set out in such a way to lead the reader through the relevant topics and has been constructed with other successful textbooks in mind. Where you feel you need a little more from another book, Willerton provides. Similarly, where a comprehensive text is required, this is a fine choice. We are confident you will find material here to develop or add to your knowledge of the topic.

- *You may be reading this book as you undertake pre-university courses such as A-level.* Both teachers and students will find Willerton's approach informed and thoughtful. We as editors worked closely with her to ensure the material is of use to you and provides not only a good solid coverage but extends your thinking and encourages you to aim higher where relevant. The Reading Guide at the end of the book tells you where different A-level specifications appear.

Whatever your area of study, or whether you are reading the book for interest, we are certain you will find it informative, engaging and useful. It may even change your life a little.

NIGEL HOLT AND ROB LEWIS
Series Editors

Chapter 1

Studying relationships: perspectives and methods

Introduction

For many people, relationships with others are one of the most important aspects, if not *the* most important aspect of life. They are often associated with our greatest feelings of happiness and when they go wrong, they can cause heartache and pain. They also occupy a good deal of our time: if we are not thinking and talking about relationships, mulling over what we said – and what we could have said – we are discussing the relationships of celebrities or watching films and reading books in which relationships are portrayed. In 2009, over 15 million people in the UK were single and over half of these were actively looking for a long-term relationship. A substantial 4.5 million UK residents visited a dating website at some point in 2008 (*Society Matters*, 2009).

In this book, we are going to explore what psychological research has discovered about personal relationships. What are relationships? A widely used definition was given by Argyle and Henderson (1985: 4) as a 'regular social encounter over a period of time'. This definition captures some important aspects of relationships: they occur over a period of time, although some are much shorter than others. They involve regular contact or interaction between two people. Personal relationships – the focus of this book – are those that are romantic and/or sexual in nature.

In this chapter we are going to introduce some of the methods psychologists have used to study relationships, along with the important perspectives in this field. These perspectives include the dominant type of social psychology, called **experimental social psychology**. We will consider some of the challenges and criticisms of this approach and the new, qualitative approaches to studying relationships that are being put forward by **critical social psychology**. We will also consider the insights into relationships offered by other branches of psychology.

This chapter will cover:
An introduction to the main perspectives in the study of personal relationships and the methods associated with each of these perspectives:
- Experimental social psychology
- Evolutionary social psychology
- Developmental social psychology
- Health psychology

The main challenges to social psychology:
- The criticisms posed by critical social psychology
- The emergence of qualitative research methods
- The need for a cross-cultural social psychology
- The need for research into understudied relationships
- Putting it all together: studying relationships

◉ Studying personal relationships

The study of personal relationships has traditionally belonged to the branch of social psychology. Social psychology has been defined as 'the scientific investigation of how the thoughts, feelings and behaviours of individuals are influenced by the actual, imagined or implied presence of others' (Allport, 1935 cited in Hogg and Vaughan, 2005: 4).

Modern social psychology includes a number of different **perspectives** (sometimes called *approaches*) that can be used to study social behaviour in general and personal relationships in particular. These perspectives are best seen as **meta-theories** as they generally include a number of smaller theories within them. Each perspective provides a specific way of looking at relationships and makes different assumptions about what aspects of people and relationships should be studied and how this might best be done. The most influential of these is *experimental social psychology*.

Relationships are not solely studied by social psychologists but also considered by many other branches of psychology as well as other disciplines such as sociology. Over the past twenty years, three branches of psychology have provided us with important insight into specific aspects of human relationships. **Evolutionary social psychology** has considered how relationships today may have their origins in the distant past. **Developmental social psychology** has looked for links between childhood experiences and later relationships in adulthood. **Health psychology** has considered the ways in which relationships affect our emotional and physical well-being. We will start by considering how each of these perspectives approaches the study of relationships.

◉ Experimental social psychology

Since the late 1970s, experimental social psychology (sometimes known as *cognitive social psychology*) has been 'the dominant perspective in social psychology' (Hogg and Vaughan, 2005: 22). It dominates most university departments, articles in journals and the research field overall. Experimental social psychology grew out of **behaviourism** in the middle of the twentieth century as researchers working within a behaviourist framework acknowledged that cognitive processes, such as thoughts and beliefs, affected how people behaved in social situations.

Experimental social psychology takes the view that people are primarily thinkers. They interpret other people and think carefully about their relationships, weighing them up and evaluating them. **Social exchange theory**, which you will meet in Chapter 5, fits into this category. Social exchange theory takes the view that people keep an eye on their relationships in a similar way to their bank accounts! They compare them with other, previous relationships in terms of enjoyment and they may also compare them with how they were in the past. People are said to weigh up the rewards or reinforcements they get from relationships as well as the bad things – such as arguments or jealousy – to see if a relationship is worth continuing or to decide whether it is time to get out.

Methods

The methods used by experimental social psychologists are **quantitative** and scientific. In the 1960s and 70s researchers made considerable use of *laboratory experiments*. Many of these early experiments were focused on very specific behaviours involved in relationships, such as initial attraction (see, for example, Byrne's 'Bogus Stranger' studies in Chapter 4) but made little attempt to study relationships in their social context or to follow them over longer periods of time to see how they developed. These methods received considerable criticism for focusing on 'isolated slices of relationships' (Miell and Dallos, 1996: 3). The realization that research needed to see how relationships changed, rather than studying them in snapshots, led to a move towards **longitudinal research** studies which followed relationships over a much longer period of time.

Today, experimental social psychologists have retained their quantitative framework but often collect data outside the laboratory setting. Methods include *field experiments*, which involve the manipulation of an independent variable in a real life setting, and **quasi-experiments**, in which naturally occurring independent variables are assessed to see their effects on dependent variables. Experimental social psychologists also make use of *correlation* to study relationships. This method involves measuring two or more variables to see if there is a pattern or relationship between them. Correlation is useful to researchers as it helps them to study areas where **random allocation** to conditions is difficult or impossible. It also avoids many of the ethical issues associated with experimentation. A detailed example of the use of correlation in relationship research is shown below.

Thinking scientifically → **A correlational approach to studying equity in couples** (Van Yperen and Buunk, 1990)

In a correlational study, researchers measure two or more variables and see if there is a pattern or relationship between them. Van Yperen and Buunk (1990) have attempted to establish if fairness in a relationship (known as *equity*) is associated with how happy and satisfied couples are with each other. Clearly, it would be difficult to study this area using a true experiment, as researchers could not randomly allocate participants to conditions by putting some in an unfair relationship. The use of quasi-experimental research would also pose some ethical problems. Couples in unfair or unhappy relationships may be reluctant to take part or distressed by being asked to think about their relationship. For these reasons, Van Yperen and Buunk carried out a study measuring feelings of equity in couples' relationships and feelings of satisfaction with the relationship. These were the two co-variables.

Van Yperen and Buunk selected a sample of 736 people, made up of 259 married couples and 109 cohabiting couples; 70% of the couples had children. Feelings of equity were measured using an anonymous questionnaire which participants were asked to complete and return without discussion with their partner. Equity was assessed at two points called Time 1 and Time 2, exactly one year apart, making this study longitudinal. Couples were also asked to indicate their satisfaction with the relationship using an eight-item scale with four positive and four negative statements at both time intervals. The scores on these two variables were correlated to see if a pattern or relationship existed between them.

Van Yperen and Buunk found that equity at Time 1 correlated with satisfaction with the relationship at Time 2. The fairer a relationship was perceived to be, the happier the couple were with it. The less fair the relationship was felt to be, the less satisfied the couples were with each other. The effect was particularly strong with women where the correlation was .44. Equity was less strongly related to happiness/satisfaction for men, with a correlation of .20.

Van Yperen and Buunk's study demonstrates many of the principles of the experimental-social approach to relationships. The researchers used quantitative methods to assess equity and satisfaction, giving each of these variables a score. The focus of the research was on what the couples thought about their relationship (cognitions). The use of correlational methods enabled the study of a sensitive area (relationship satisfaction) without researcher intervention or manipulation.

Social psychologist Michael Argyle is a strong supporter of experimental approaches to study relationships. He argues that 'experimental approaches ... may be the best, sometimes the only way to test hypotheses and show causal influences' (1996: 344). Some recent research studies also make use of **triangulation**, the utilization of a range of different methods to gain a rich insight into a topic. John Gottman's Love lab methodology (which you can read more about in Chapter 5, Regulating relationships) shows how multiple methods can help us to understand the complexity of personal relationships.

◉ Evolutionary social psychology

Evolutionary social psychology is one of the more recent developments within social psychology (Hogg and Vaughan, 2005). This perspective approaches the study of relationships by assuming that attraction, sexual desire and relationships have their origins in the evolutionary past. Evolutionary social psychologists (sometimes called sociobiologists) draw on the ideas proposed by Charles Darwin (1871) of **natural selection** and **sexual selection**. Behaviours or bodily features that brought advantages to our ancestors in terms of survival or attraction of mates were likely to be passed on to their offspring, who would inherit these advantages. These behaviours and bodily features may continue to exist in modern women and men today. Evolutionary social psychologists begin by observations of behaviour and then attempt to infer how and why such behaviours existed and aided survival and/or reproduction in the past.

Methods

Rather than being associated with one single methodological approach, evolutionary social psychology is characterized by the use of a wide range of methods. Because researchers cannot go back to see how our ancestors lived in the past, they test their hypotheses using many types of evidence, in a similar way to a detective (Clegg, 2007). Researchers may use quasi-experimental methods, comparing the sexual behaviours of men and women today, then attempt to devise explanations as to how and why such behaviours may have evolved; an approach sometimes called *reverse engineering*. They may also use a comparative approach, comparing humans to closely related primates such as chimpanzees. Cross-cultural studies are also extremely informative: if a behaviour or preference of some kind occurs fairly universally across cultures it is reasonable to assume that it is inbuilt and passed on genetically. An example of one universal preference is in the age gap between men and women: in a study of 37 different cultures, Buss (1989) found that men universally preferred younger women – not surprising as fertility in women is linked to youth. Researchers may study societies who continue to follow a hunter-gatherer lifestyle similar to that of our ancestors, such as the !Kung San of the Kalahari Desert. An example of a study examining the preference for female body shape in a hunter-gatherer society is detailed below.

Featured method → **Studies of hunter-gatherer societies (Randall, 1995)**

Are the preferences for female body shape the same across different cultures? In western societies such as the UK, a slim body shape is currently considered attractive. In order to test if this preference is universal, Randall (1995) has studied the preferences in different parts of the world where food is scarce. In one hunter-gatherer tribe based in the Sahara Desert, young women are deliberately 'fattened up' in order to make them marriageable. The Tuareg tribe of the Sahara Desert prefer women bordering on a size considered obese in western societies. Tuareg parents force-feed their young daughters with milk-rich diets to make them gain weight and increase their value (Randall, 1995).

This study indicates that preferences for particular female body shapes are not the same across all cultures. However, it would appear that preferences *are* finely 'tuned' to the specific environment. In places where food is easily available such as the US and UK, a slimmer female body is preferred but in regions where food is scarce (for example sub-Saharan Africa) a larger body shape is desired as this indicates a well-nourished girl who is more likely to bear children.

◉ Developmental social psychology

Another important perspective in the field of personal relationships is developmental social psychology. Developmental social psychologists are interested in examining possible links between childhood relationships (or attachments) and adult romantic relationships. Building on the influential **attachment** theory presented by John Bowlby (1969), this perspective takes the view that early relationships between children and their caregivers (most often parents) create templates or **internal working models** for later relationships. Children who have relatively **secure attachments** with parents are more likely to approach adult relationships with trust and a sense that they are loveable than those with insecure attachments.

Methods

Developmental social psychologists use a range of methods to measure childhood and adult attachments. Observational methods were originally used by Mary Ainsworth in the *Strange Situation* (1971) to measure young children's responses to separation from the mother-figure and distress at contact from a stranger. However, measuring adult attachments is rather more problematic. Although adults can be asked about their relationships, their answers may show the effects of **social desirability** and many people are likely to tell researchers what they think they want to hear. Adults are aware when they are being observed and may act very differently. If they are asked to recall memories of relationships with parents these may be fuzzy or vague.

One method that has been devised to 'get round' these problems of self-report is the **adult attachment interview** (AAI) devised by Mary Main and colleagues working in the United States (Main, Kaplan and Cassidy, 1985). In the AAI, what is said is less important than *how* people talk about their relationships and the kind of narrative they provide.

Featured method → **The adult attachment interview**
(Main, Kaplan and Cassidy, 1985)

The AAI looks at *how* the individual talks about their past rather than *what* is said. The AAI consists of a standardized interview in which a set of questions explore how adults describe the relationships they had with their parents. The focus of the analysis is not on the content of the interview but on the way the individual talks about their past relationships. The interview is coded by trained observers who look at a number of features:

- The structure of the account (whether the talk is like a story or rambles, returning to the same issues several times)
- The amount of detail included
- The internal consistency of the narrative (Are there contradictory statements?)
- The coherence of the narrative (Do the points fit together?).

Using this method, Main and colleagues have identified three basic ways in which people talk about relationships with their parents:

1 *A dismissing narrative:* takes place where the person gives little detail and recalls events in a bland and unemotional way. They may also give the impression that the past is not very important to them.

2 *An autonomous narrative:* here the person talks about both the past and the present. The interview contains depth and detail of both positive and negative experiences

3 *A preoccupied narrative:* in this narrative the individual talks in a long, often rambling style without clear structure. Past events are often described with strong feeling or are dwelled upon. These feelings continue to seem strong in the present and the speaker may appear to be 'stuck' in events from the past.

The AAI is an extremely useful tool as it is relatively free from demand characteristics: while people may claim to have had a happy childhood, the coding of the interview may suggest that an adult could be classified as insecure from their narrative despite the claims. You can read more about this method of studying adult attachments in Chapter 3.

👁 Health psychology

The final branch of psychology that we will draw on is that of health psychology. Health psychologists are interested in the effects of relationships on well-being. It may seem pretty obvious that relationships have effects: after all, most of us know how great we can feel when important relationships go well and we may have also experienced the negative effects on mood when relationships are going badly. However, a range of research has begun to demonstrate just how important relationships can be, not just to emotional well-being but also to our physical health.

How can we investigate the effects of relationships? One method used by health psychologists is **epidemiology**, the statistical study of how long people live and when they die. Epidemiological studies show remarkable findings: people who get married and stay married live longer than those who are separated, divorced or never married (for example Angier, 1990; Ross, Mirowsky and Goldsteen, 1990; Sbarra and Nietert, 2009). However statistical methods do not tell us *why* such effects occur. For this reason, health psychologists have devised methods that make use of physiological or **material data** and that provide precise and detailed explanations of the underlying mechanisms which link relationships and health.

Featured method → **Physiological data** (Kiecolt-Glaser et al., 1993)

Kiecolt-Glaser and colleagues (1993) have examined the immediate physiological effects on the body when couples are instructed to have an argument! In this study, 90 newly married couples had blood samples taken on the hour from 8.00am in the morning until 10.00pm at night. These samples were pooled to provide a measurement of six key hormones related to stress. The couples were asked to discuss an area of conflict in their relationship in the middle of the morning to assess changes to stress hormones. These could be compared to the baseline levels that had been established from the hourly blood tests.

Kiecolt-Glaser et al. found that the female members of the couples produced elevated levels of two particular stress hormones during the argument/discussion, **cortisol** and *norepinephrine*. Production was highest in those women whose partners responded to the conflict by withdrawal or unwillingness to discuss the problem. In fact, arguments accounted for substantial variations of hormones (between 24% and 29%) across the day in women.

In contrast, the men in Kiecolt-Glaser et al.'s study did not show elevated levels of stress hormones levels in response to the argument. Subsequent studies have shown that women's levels of cortisol elevate during an argument and remain high more than half an hour after the argument has ended, leaving the participants literally stewing in stress hormones (Fehm-Wolfsdorf, Groth, Kaiser and Hahlweg, 1999). It seems that women may be wired to respond to conflict.

Physiological data provides an important contribution to our understanding of how exactly relationships may produce longer-term effects on health. When short-term studies like these demonstrate such clear effects, it is not surprising that unhappy relationships might affect health. In Chapter 8, we will consider these methods and findings in detail.

Summary

- Relationships are studied using different perspectives
- The experimental social perspective uses quantitative methods including experimentation and correlation
- This perspective dominates most journals and university departments
- Evolutionary social psychology is a multi-method enterprise that attempts to establish how relationships may have been affected by natural and sexual selection
- Developmental social psychologists examine how early relationships (attachments) link to later adult relationships
- Measuring adult attachments is more challenging than measuring attachments in babies
- Health psychologists establish how relationships affect emotional and physical well-being

◉ The 'crisis' in social psychology

Up to the 1970s, most research into relationships operated within the scientific tradition using quantitative methods. However, the 1970s saw a wave of criticisms of social psychology. These criticisms were focused around a number of different areas:

1 *The methodology adopted:* a wave of criticism was focused on the use of highly scientific methods such as experiments. It was argued that these were inadequate at capturing the complexity of human relationships leading to distorted and misleading findings. Critics argued that these methods focused on fragments of relationships and failed to consider how relationships grow and change.

2 *The biased nature of research into relationships:* many of the studies at this time were carried out in western countries (generally North America) using mainly white, middle-class, heterosexual student participants. There were few research studies that examined relationships in other cultures or between gay and lesbian couples. In fact, many kinds of relationships were ignored or invisible and were simply understudied.

3 *The reductionistic nature of research studies:* critics argued that social psychology had focused too much on individual characteristics and had ignored the importance of social influences. For example, explanations of relationship breakdown (splitting up) had often looked at the personalities of the two people involved but had overlooked other factors such as how the couple communicated or the important influence of social networks such as friends and family.

Challenges to methods: critical social psychology and the use of qualitative methods

This crisis led to a split in modern social psychology into two opposing 'camps'. Traditional social psychologists took on board many of these criticisms but continued to work within a quantitative framework using correlations, field experiments and longitudinal studies. In contrast, critical social psychologists rejected quantitative methods and devised new ways of studying social psychology and relationships using **qualitative methods**. This split led to a range of new social psychological perspectives, perhaps the most influential of which is **discursive social psychology**.

Discursive social psychologists are interested in the importance of language in helping us to understand social relationships. They assume that people draw on ideas taken from their culture to talk about relationships (Lucey, 2007). Think, for example about the explanations 'I broke up with her because the relationship wasn't going anywhere' or 'She was just using me'. These ideas draw on commonly held views about relationships in western culture: relationships should grow and change rather than stay static, they are like a journey that two people embark on together and they should involve mutual effort. Cultural concepts of this nature are called **interpretative repertoires**. Discursive social psychologists argue that we use them to make sense of our relationships as well as to persuade other people that our relationship decisions and views are justifiable/right. For this reason, discursive psychologists choose to study talk from interviews, diaries and conversations.

There are many different kinds of discourse analysis which are outside our interest here. However, the study below by Simon, Eder and Evans (1992) demonstrates some of the principles of a discursive approach to relationships.

Featured method → **Qualitative approach to studying relationships** (Simon, Eder and Evans, 1992)

Simon, Eder and Evans (1992) studied groups of young girls aged between 11 and 14 years old in a school in mid-western America. The aim of their study was to look at the ideas expressed by the girls about love and romance. The data was collected with minimal researcher involvement: the researchers used naturally occurring group discussions, field notes and some in-depth group interviews. This produced qualitative data, which was transcribed and analysed using **discourse analysis**.

The researchers looked at how the girls expressed common views or 'interpretative repertoires' taken from their wider culture. These included norms, for example that romantic feelings should only be directed towards boys – not girls – and that you should only have romantic feelings for one boy at a time. From this, the researchers were able to see how the girls argued about these, how they negotiated the norms or rules and how they corrected or 'policed' those who disagreed, often using humour and teasing. If girls continued to disagree or challenge the norms, confrontation was used.

The researchers argue that girls acquire cultural knowledge and ideas about love from talking together, listening to adults talk and from other cultural tools such as television and music lyrics (think about how influential the American sitcom *Friends* continues to be!) These exert powerful influences that are often accepted without much questioning in younger teenagers.

The qualitative approach taken here is very different to those we have looked at in the social–cognitive perspective. Researchers reject the use of measurement and scales. They aim to use minimal involvement with their participants and try to capture natural conversations which are uncontaminated by the process of study. Qualitative methods of this nature can provide rich insights into how people think and talk about their relationships. You will meet a range of qualitative research studies across the different chapters of this book. Note how qualitative researchers aim to examine and capture experiences – often using relatively small samples of participants – rather than to look for causes of behaviour.

◉ The need for cross-cultural social psychology

As well as the methodological critique posed by critical social psychology, other critics drew attention to the culturally biased nature of research on relationships. Although relationships take place in all areas of the world and 'people just about everywhere fall in love and have similar, intense emotional feelings about the person they love' (Goodwin, 2005: 614), most of the research into relationships in the 1970s was carried out in western, industrialized societies such as North America, Europe and Australia. Findings of these studies were used to devise models of relationships that were assumed to apply fairly universally across the world.

However, in the 1960s and 70s researchers challenged this assumption as emerging evidence demonstrated large cultural variations in basic human behaviours, social psychological processes and relationships in particular (Hogg and Vaughan, 2005: 614). These findings led to claims that social psychology was **culture bound** and **culture blind**:

- *The culture bound criticism:* this criticism rested on the fact that research studies largely collected their data from a narrow cultural background focusing on middle-class, white, Americans. As Goodwin (2005: 614) says, 'we know a great deal about North American sophomores (undergraduate students) but precious little about cultural diversity in relationships even within multi-cultural Western societies'. The data collected in these studies has been used to build many influential theories such as **equity theory**, making these also culture bound.

- *The culture blind criticism:* this criticism rested on the claim that many of the theories of relationships had received little testing outside the culture in which they were produced.

An interest in cross-cultural psychology grew and flowered in the late 1960s and early 1970s with the publication of the first psychological journals devoted to cross-cultural research. Many of these research studies were still rather limited and have been described by Goodwin (1999) as 'fishing trips'; one-off investigations into cultural practices, lacking systematic methods of inquiry. He argues that most research studies from this period fitted into one of three types:

1 Studies carried out by overseas students visiting the 'academic power blocks' of North America and Europe and comparing relationships in their home culture with western relationships
2 Studies carried out by western psychologists using short visits overseas
3 Studies that attempted to test if western theories/findings applied in a different culture.

As you can read in Chapter 7, the study of cultural variations in relationships has come a long way since then. Cross-cultural social psychologists have established a range of important factors that affect how relationships are structured, formed and governed in different parts of the world and in different religious groups. These studies have shown us that many of the assumptions about relationships that were believed to be universal are, in reality, 'true' in very few places of the world but are simply western practices. Take for example the assumption that relationships can be ended when a couple are unhappy: while divorce is technically available in most countries of the world, the proportion/percentage of couples who end their marriage varies dramatically across cultures. As we shall see in Chapter 7, much of the more recent cross-cultural research is carried out by psychologists living and working within the culture they study. One of the largest challenges facing cross-cultural work is the rapid westernization of many Asian countries.

◉ The need for a psychology of same-sex relationships

Another important criticism related to the narrow range of relationships studied. Until the late 1970s, most research studies focused on heterosexual couples and ignored relationships formed between same-sex couples, leaving them understudied. Any research that did exist viewed homosexual relationships as abnormal or pathological, leading Kitzinger et al. (1998) to refer to gay relationships as an 'invisible minority' in research. Many of the models and theories of relationships developed at this time assumed that homosexual and heterosexual relationships were similar and the same principles could be applied to both. Kitzinger and Coyle (1995) have been vocal critics of these assumptions, arguing that research of this nature attempts to 'force lesbian and gay lifestyles into those patterns supposed typical of heterosexuals'. They argue that much of the research is inappropriate as gay men and women 'confront different challenges, both socially and psychologically' (Kitzinger et al., 1998: 530) and operate relationships via their own rules, which are different to those of heterosexual relationships.

Since the early 1990s a steady volume of research findings have begun to lead to greater understanding of same-sex relationships. The American Psychological Association (APA) and the British Psychological Society (BPS) have both established divisions devoted exclusively to the study of gay and lesbian psychology. Like the early cross-cultural studies we have just considered, research studies have not been without criticism. Kurdek (2005) has argued that many research studies have used relatively small, convenience samples, which made it easy to collect data but which reduces the ability of researchers to generalize – a criticism we will examine in detail later in this book. What are some of the unique features of gay and lesbian relationships?

A lack of gender differences

One inevitable feature of heterosexual relationships relates to differences between men and women. As you will see in Chapters 5 and 6, men and women in general show differences in communication patterns, styles and methods of dealing with conflict. In fact, the idea that men and women are different species is engrained in popular culture with best-sellers such as *Men are from Mars and Women are from Venus* (John Gray, 1992) dominating the shelves at many retailers. These gender differences do not exist in relationships comprising two men or two women. In same-sex relationships, there is no gender basis for deciding how roles are allocated around the household, who puts the washing in or who puts the oil in the car. Each of these tasks must be allocated via discussion and negotiation often leading to a stronger feeling of equality within same-sex relationships (Dunne, 1997).

Kurdek (1995) explored how household tasks are allocated within both homosexual and heterosexual relationships. A study of 314 couples found that lesbians were likely to allocate tasks equally, sharing and completing them together, whereas gay men were likely to balance out the tasks, splitting them up equally but specializing in different areas. In contrast, the division of labour in heterosexual couples often led to conflict, with one person (usually the woman) doing the bigger share. Similarly, Gottman et al. (2003) explored how couples deal with conflict and arguments and discovered that gay and lesbian couples are more likely to discuss differences positively and warmly than heterosexual couples who often degenerate into demand/withdrawal patterns. Kurdek (1995) is correct in saying that we can learn a good deal about how to run relationships by studying same-sex couples!

Less support for relationships

A second important set of differences arise in the acceptance of gay relationships within the immediate social network such as family and within wider society. In some countries such as Belgium, civil marriages allow gay couples to legalize their union and provide them with some of the legal benefits of marriage, but many other western countries do not recognize same-sex relationships in any legal sense. One consequence of this is that financial interdependence between gay couples is much less likely than between heterosexual couples, as there are few legal opportunities to sort things out should the relationship break down. Related to this is the lack of family support, involvement and help for many gay couples. Kurdek (2005: 252) calls this 'a unique stressor' which applies acutely to same-sex couples. You can read more about this in Chapters 5, 6 and 8.

While there are differences between homosexual and heterosexual relationships, there are also similarities. Studies have indicated that a similar pattern of happiness and satisfaction is shown in long-term relationships regardless of sexuality. Relationships – both gay and straight – in western cultures start with high levels of happiness which decrease over the first few years. Kurdek (2005) argues that researchers should investigate the 'life course' of gay and lesbian relationships, to see how they progress from casual to committed and to identify which variables and factors are unique to them. In order to do this, much larger representative samples will be essential.

◉ Exploring other kinds of understudied relationships

Another recent development in the field of social relationships has been the diverse ways in which relationships begin and operate. Development of communication technologies, including SMS texting, internet dating sites, chat rooms and social networking sites has provided a new arena in which relationships can develop. 'Virtual' relationships have become incredibly prolific as we noted at the start of this chapter. One dating site aimed at young Asians, Shaadi.com, has over 15 million subscribers and around 4.5 million UK residents used an internet dating site in 2008, making this a rapidly growing area. An important feature of virtual relationships is their diversity. Some relationships begin online then move to a face-to-face format. Others stay entirely online and some may start in a face-to-face way then continue online via a social networking site such as Facebook. Like same-sex relationships, computer mediated relationships operate by their own set of rules and systems which are different to those formed face to face. People often meet and get to know a great deal about each other via chatting before meeting face to face. They may have little idea what the other person looks like apart from a carefully chosen photograph on a profile. We will examine research in this growing area in Chapter 4.

◉ Putting it all together: studying relationships

The above discussion has indicated that our understanding of relationships is enhanced by many different branches of psychology. It has also demonstrated that the study of relationships is a multi-method enterprise: researchers choose methods depending on the kinds of questions or hypotheses they wish to answer. Most of the theories and research studies you will meet in this book fit within one of the perspectives we have met here. We will start by examining the evolutionary basis for human relationships in Chapter 2 before moving on to consider the insights offered from developmental social psychology into the importance of early attachments in Chapter 3. Chapters 4 and 5 (formation and regulation of relationships) are considered from an experimental social perspective and Chapter 6 uses insights from all perspectives to examine what we know about relationship breakdown. In Chapter 7, we explore how relationships vary in different societies and cultures across the world. Finally, in Chapter 8, we will consider some of the important insights from health psychology about the effects of relationships on our emotional and physical well-being. In each of these chapters you can read more about diversity in relationships.

Summary

- Traditional social psychology was criticized in the 1980s, leading to a crisis and split between experimental and critical social psychology
- Experimental methods were seen as reductionist and lacking in validity
- Critical social psychologists use qualitative research methods to investigate the complexities of human relationships
- Discursive social psychology is an influential perspective which uses discourse analysis
- Social psychology was also criticized for being culture bound, culture blind and heterosexist
- Cross-cultural researchers have demonstrated that relationships are organized very differently in different cultures
- Research into same-sex relationships has identified important differences from heterosexual relationships, as well as unique features
- The study of relationships is a multi-method enterprise

⊙ Further reading

An excellent European social psychology textbook is *Social Psychology* (4th edition, 2005) by Michael Hogg and Graham Vaughan, published by Pearson.

An extremely readable introduction to critical social psychology and qualitative methods is given by Brendan Gough and Majella McFadden (2001) *Critical social Psychology*: Basingstoke, Palgrave Macmillan.

You can read more about cross-cultural social psychology in *Personal Relationships Across Cultures* (Robin Goodwin, 1999) published by Routledge.

Chapter 2

An evolutionary perspective on human relationships

⊙ Introduction

In this chapter, we shall consider how the sexual preferences, behaviours and relationships of women and men today may have been shaped by forces in the evolutionary past. The evolutionary perspective on relationships argues that the behaviours we see in people today have their origins in the past and exist because they conveyed advantages to our distant ancestors. This perspective draws from the ideas of Charles Darwin on **natural selection** and **sexual selection**. We shall start by examining the characteristics of the environment in which our ancestors lived before moving on to consider how these might have shaped the sexual preferences and behaviours we see in men and women today. We will then move on to consider two theories that offer competing explanations for these differences, Trivers' (1972) **parental investment theory** and Buss and Schmitt's (1993) **sexual strategies theory**. Underlying the evolutionary perspective is the belief 'that human cognitive abilities and behaviours are the product of a long period of evolution' (Clegg, 2007: 107).

This chapter will cover:
- The evolutionary concepts of natural and sexual selection, and how these influence sexual attraction, behaviour and relationships
- Why men and women find different physical features attractive in partners
- Differences in sexual behaviours shown by men and women

- Evolutionary explanations of these differences offered by parental investment theory (Trivers, 1972) and sexual strategies theory (Buss and Schmidt, 1993)

The effects of social isolation

Like most people, you have probably experienced feelings of acute loneliness at different times in your life. Perhaps you have moved school or house to a new area where you did not know anyone. Studies of voluntary isolation have demonstrated to us just how powerful the need to form relationships with other people really is. In 1938, Admiral Richard E. Byrd volunteered to spend a period of six months alone at an Antarctic weather station to document climate. Although he had radio contact with the base station, he was unable to see or talk face to face with another person. Byrd began to feel extremely lonely, lost and isolated after three weeks and soon imagined he was not alone. After three months he became depressed and experienced hallucinations and bizarre delusional ideas. If you have seen the film, *Cast Away* you may recall how Tom Hanks dealt with his state of involuntary isolation by the creation of a volley ball (named Wilson) as a friend! Such studies of isolation are rare and clearly focus on unique individuals. However, they point to the inevitable conclusion: isolation and loneliness are extremely unpleasant states which most people work hard to avoid. People need people.

Lives as hunter-gatherers

Think, for a moment or two, about the lives of your ancestors thousands of years ago. It is widely agreed that the last common ancestor of both apes and humans was a species called australopithecines (or Southern apes) who lived between 5 and 7 million years ago (MYA). The multi-regional hypothesis of modern human origins claims that humans emerged between one and 1.5 million years ago from a descendant of these apes known as Homo Erectus (upright man) and those different groups evolved separately in different parts of the world. In contrast, the 'Out of Africa' hypothesis (Stringer and McKie, 1996) suggests that all humans share a common ancestor who lived in Africa much more recently between 100,000 and 200,000 years ago. This group is thought to have emerged from Africa crossing land bridges into other continents to colonize different parts of the world leading to the various human races we can see today.

An important time in human evolutionary history is thought to have been the period between about 40,000 and 10,000 years ago, which is known as the **Environment of Evolutionary Adaptation** (EEA). During this period humans lived a hunter-gatherer lifestyle. They gathered berries and fruits and hunted animals for food. In order to survive in these challenging environments, individuals needed to ensure regular supplies of water, and find shelter from the elements and protection from predators. In addition they needed to defend supplies from competitors. Offspring struggled to thrive and many died. The tasks that were essential for survival – tracking and hunting large animals, finding mates, caring for offspring and protecting against predators – were made much easier for the individual who lived within a small social group and it is thought that early humans probably lived in small social groups of about 150 people, a figure known as **Dunbar's number**.

Evolutionary psychologists argue that the human mind has been shaped by processes operating during the hunter-gatherer period. The amount of time that has passed since then has been relatively short in terms of evolution and it is likely that many of the traits and behaviours seen today may date back to that period. Unlike other kinds of psychologists, evolutionists are interested in why behaviours exist today and the functions they may have served in the past. Many of the behaviours we can see today may have been shaped by the processes of natural selection and sexual selection.

Natural and sexual selection

The precise mechanisms that led to the evolution or gradual change of species are called natural and sexual selection. According to the principle of natural selection (Darwin, 1859), members of a species vary in appearance (which we call 'morphology') and in behaviour. For example, a look around your fellow students will demonstrate variations in height, body shape, hair and eye colour as well as in personality characteristics. Within any environment, members of species compete for access to physical resources such as food and shelter. They also attempt to avoid danger from predators. If a variation in behaviour or morphology produces an advantage in this competition, this should enable that individual to survive more successfully than those who do not possess the feature or behaviour. For example, those members of a species who can run faster would be more likely to escape from predation than slower runners. Natural selection can therefore be seen as selection imposed on individuals by the environmental conditions operating in a particular time and place. If the variation that led to increased survival is passed on in genes, offspring may inherit the feature which produced the advantage. Over a period of time, most members of the species will come to possess this bodily feature or behaviour. This process is known as natural selection.

Darwin was initially puzzled by bodily features in animals such as the peacock's train: this elaborate and beautiful tail appeared to offer no apparent survival value to the owner. In fact, the peacock's tail made survival less likely as it prevented effective flight and escape from predators and made the peacock extremely conspicuous. However, observation showed that peacocks with long and glorious trains were preferred by peahens who would select males to mate with on the basis of the size of their train. This led Darwin (1871) to propose an additional concept to natural selection, which was the idea of sexual selection. Darwin argued that bodily features (such as the peacock's tail) existed because they were valued by potential partners (female peahens) and deemed attractive, leading to increased opportunities for mating and greater reproductive success.

We can identify two types of sexual selection. **Intra-sexual selection** takes place when members of one sex (often males) compete for access to the other sex in various ways including fighting. Characteristics that make a male more successful in this fight (for example a larger or heavier body) are likely to be passed to any offspring. In contrast, **inter-sexual selection** occurs when members of one sex (often females) choose mates from the other sex. Females may choose mates for a range of different reasons: these could be because they appear healthy and will pass on good genes to potential offspring. Alternatively they may choose males they think will protect and help to raise potential offspring. Finally their preferences may be purely arbitrary: they may simply find certain characteristics sexy. Sexual selection primarily takes place by male competition and female choice.

A study carried out by Lycett and Dunbar (2000) has suggested that the modern equivalent of a peacock's beautiful train may well be possessions such as a classy mobile phone! Lycett and Dunbar carried out an observational study over a period of four months in Liverpool, watching and recording the ways in which men and women used their phones in cafes and bars. They found that while women usually kept phones in their bags, men placed theirs on the table in front of them, displaying their phone for all to see in a similar way to the peacock's display of his train. We shall consider why such a display of wealth by males could offer reproductive advantages in attracting potential mates later on in this chapter.

How has sexual selection led to physical differences between men and women?

Think for a moment about the ways in which men and women differ in appearance. Some of these differences such as length and style of hair are a matter of personal choice and can be changed. But others are systematic differences between most men and most women. An example of this is an increased amount of facial and bodily hair in men. Differences in bodily features between males and females of a species are known as **sexual dimorphism**. What are the main differences between men's and women's appearance? On average, men are taller than women by about 8–10% and weigh between 20 and 40% more. Men are able to grow impressive beards and generally have deeper pitched voices. Men and women also differ in body shape: after puberty, the female figure is curvy, tending towards an 'hour glass' shape, with breasts, hips and a waist whereas men have more muscular upper bodies, wider chests and slim hips leading to a V-shaped outline. These differences appear to have little to do with survival value as women and children survive perfectly well without beards and hairy chests, suggesting that these characteristics may have been sexually, rather than naturally selected.

How might these differences have evolved through the process of sexual selection? Barber (1995) argues that physical differences between males and females of species have been magnified through competition with rivals (intra-sexual selection) or through attraction of mates (inter-sexual selection) Males who were bigger and heavier were more likely to succeed over smaller rivals when fighting for access to females and this may have led to increases in male height and weight. In fact, studies support this claim: taller men in Poland are more likely to have children than shorter men (Pawlowski, Dunbar and Lipowitz, 2000). Barber (1995) found that women judge men with beards to be more attractive than clean shaven men and they prefer men with muscular upper bodies, suggesting female choice (inter-sexual selection) may also play a part.

Sexual selection and attraction

What do men find attractive in potential female partners? Cunningham (1986) explored the importance of different facial features in men's views of female beauty. Using photos of 50 women and varying the size of features including eyes, nose and chin, he found that men were most attracted to women with large eyes, small noses and chins, features which are found in the faces of young children. In addition, prominent cheek-bones and narrow cheeks were also seen as attractive along with dilated pupils and a large smile. In terms of ideal body shape, women are judged as most attractive when their figure fits an 'hour glass' shape of large breasts and slim waists. Singh (1993) found that a waist–hip ratio (WHR) of about .7 was deemed to be an attractive female body shape across a range of different cultures. This preference exists despite cultural differences for curvier or slimmer body shapes.

How might these preferences have been sexually selected? Many of the features that make women attractive to men are those associated with youth, such as large eyes and a small nose or chin. In women, youth is strongly linked to fertility as fertility declines rapidly after the age of about 35. Men who preferred women with youthful features were likely to have had greater reproductive success in the past. Similarly, men who preferred to mate with women with a WHR of around .7 may have been more successful in reproductive terms, as this body shape is highly correlated with fertility and reproductive health (Singh, 1993). In fact, a curvy shape denotes clearly to a man that the female has reached puberty and is unlikely to be already pregnant.

What do women find attractive in potential male partners? In males, the ideal WHR is around 0.85 to 0.9, which signifies a tapering figure from wide shoulders down to narrowing hips. Some studies of male attractiveness (Cunningham, Barbee and Pike, 1990) have indicated that women prefer 'rugged' men with masculine features including strong jaws, small eyes and ridged eyebrows. However, not all studies have agreed on this. Waynforth, Delwardia and Camm (2005) showed women photos of 45 men with varying facial features and found no overall preference for highly masculine features. However, when women were asked about their current **mate preferences**, it was found that those who were interested in short-term relationships found highly masculine faces attractive.

The features that signify attractiveness in men's face are those associated with maturity and social dominance. Female preferences for these types of features may have evolved as older men generally possessed more resources, which aided the survival of offspring. Masculine features are associated with higher levels of the male hormone testosterone (Cunningham et al., 1990) and a preference for masculine facial features may have been linked with a mate who was good at defending the resources needed to maintain a family unit. However, highly masculine men may be a double blessing: a study by Waynforth (2001) found that women judged very attractive men as more likely to cheat on their partners than moderately attractive men.

Some factors, for example longer than average legs, are attractive to both men and women. Pawlowski and Sorokowski (2008) asked a sample of 218 males and females to rank the attractiveness of seven pictures of men and seven of women, which were digitally altered for leg length. He found that in both sexes 5% longer legs than average were seen as the most attractive. Using computer manipulated images, Bruce and Young (1998) have found that there is a preference for symmetrical faces in both men and women. These preferences may have been selected because they are associated with good health: long legs indicate good nutrition in childhood and symmetrical faces are thought to signify 'good' genes, which provide a strong resistance to illness.

Sexual selection and mate preference

Sexual selection has helped us to understand why certain physical features may make someone attractive. However, sexual selection also plays a wider role in mate selection or the choice of long-term partners. We have already noted that those who left behind more offspring in the past would have greater **reproductive success** than those who had fewer surviving offspring. Studies relating to mate preferences have yielded some strikingly consistent findings about which factors are deemed as desirable in potential partners. Important factors include age and height, humour, social skills, personality, income or status.

An easy way of establishing mate preferences is to look at personal column adverts (PCAs) in newspapers or on dating websites. Over the past couple of decades the use of Lonely Hearts adverts has increased dramatically and these adverts provide 'a neatly encapsulated vignette of a person's mate choice preferences' (Barrett, Dunbar and Lycett, 2002:

96). Studies using PCAs have yielded strikingly consistent findings. A study carried out by Pawlowski and Dunbar (1999/2001) examined adverts placed by 454 heterosexual women and 445 men in *The Observer* Sunday newspaper. **Content analysis** was used to measure reference to key terms indicating resources, commitment, physical attractiveness, sex, interests and charm. Consistent with previous research findings (for example Kenrick and Keefe, 1992), Pawlowski and Dunbar found that 24% of women sought male partners who indicated wealth or status and 35% of women referred to commitment in potential partners. About one third of women (33%) requested a physically attractive partner, and social skills, such as a good sense of humour, were important to over half the female sample (52%).

In contrast, just under half of male advertisers (43%) sought an attractive partner and a similar proportion were interested in the social skills of their partners. Male advertisers put much less emphasis on the other categories. These preferences are still shown in older people seeking partners even when they are past reproductive age (Sears-Roberts, Alterovitz and Mendelsohn, 2009) and they also apply across a range of different places. In an analysis of studies in 37 different cultures, Buss (1989) found that across all cultures, women put a greater value on the status or resources of potential male partners, whereas men put more emphasis on the physical appearance of female partners.

Age is also important in mate preferences. Most advertisers in Pawlowski and Dunbar's studies stated their own age ('Male early thir-ties') and requested an age range in a partner ('seeks female aged 24 to 30'). Typically, women sought male partners who were slightly older than themselves and men sought women who were slightly younger. As men got older, their requests for female partners specified women who were still of reproductive age, often with men in their late forties seeking women in their late twenties or early thirties.

Height also emerges as a theme in PCAs. Across all cultures, women prefer a male partner who is taller than themselves. Frederick et al. (2008) examined 2000 adverts and found that men and women stated their own height and most specified a relationship in which the male was taller. This appeared more important to women than men: 23% of men would date a taller woman but only 4% of women would accept a smaller man.

Thinking scientifically → **Content analysis of personal column adverts**

Personal column adverts (PCAs) provide an easy opportunity for evolutionary psychologists to collect data relating to partner choice. The most common method used to analyse this kind of data is content analysis: this quantitative method involves counting the number of references made to particular criteria in each advert, to assess the characteristics offered to attract partners and sought in potential respondents. Each term used is placed into one of several categories, for example references to own house/car may be classified into wealth/resources, whereas characteristics such as reliable or dependable may be classified as demonstrating commitment. Typically, adverts indicate that a relatively small number of different categories are used: in Pawlowski and Dunbar's (2001) study, which we considered earlier, six categories were used to classify data. Once data has been collected and classified, comparisons can be made to examine similarities and differences between subgroups of people such as males and females or gay and straight advertisers.

Of course, there is no guarantee that PCAs are truthful. However, people who place adverts are clearly seeking a relationship of some kind. Others have criticized analysis of adverts by arguing that those who advertise for partners may not be representative of the population generally and may form an atypical sample. However, Barrett, Dunbar and Lycett (2002) argue that the increase in numbers of people placing Lonely Hearts adverts can be explained by a number of factors including increased social mobility, which leaves many young people adrift in unfamiliar cities where they know very few people, and the increase in thirty to forty pluses seeking a relationship after divorce or separation.

Summary

- In the EEA, humans are thought to have lived a hunter–gatherer lifestyle in small social groups
- Natural selection has led to the preservation of behaviours and bodily features which increase survival
- Sexual selection has preserved behaviours and bodily features which lead to increased reproductive success
- Sexual selection may have shaped physical differences between men and women as well as differences in attraction and mate preferences

◉ Human reproductive behaviours

As well as differences in mate preference, we can also consider differences in behaviours of men and women related to sexuality and mating. There are many similarities between men's and women's sexual behaviour. Both men and women have short-term relationships (affairs, flings or one-night stands) and both form lasting relationships in which they produce and raise offspring. Both sexes fall in and out of love and experience sexual jealousy. However, there are also some fairly clear differences in sexual behaviour and style, which have been documented by research studies. It is possible that these differences may originate in sexual selection: however, as we shall consider later, cultural factors such as religious practices may also contribute to these differences.

One of the differences between men and women is in the demand for sexual variety. Studies have demonstrated that men tend to seek and desire greater numbers of sexual partners than women and are more likely to use pornography or pay for sex with prostitutes. The Kinsey Report of American Sexual Behaviour (Kinsey, Pomeroy and Martin 1948/1953) indicated that around 70% of American men had visited a prostitute at some time compared to very few women. A glance around a sample of top shelf magazines such as *FHM*, *Zoo* and *Nuts* indicates that most are aimed at men: in fact, glossy magazines aimed at women more often show pictures of women celebrities than of naked men! Buss and Schmidt (1993) asked a sample of 75 men and 73 women how many sexual partners they would ideally like over a series of time intervals including the next two years, the next decade and their lifetime. They found that on average, men would like eight partners over the next two years compared to women's one partner. Over a lifetime, the averages were respectively 18 (men) and between 4 and 5 (women). At each time interval, men expressed a preference for significantly more partners than women.

A second well-documented difference is the tendency to engage in casual sex (Buss and Schmidt, 1993). On balance, men tend to be much more likely to have short-term relationships or one-night stands than women. This tendency was demonstrated beautifully in a series of studies carried out by Clark and Hatfield (1989) on US university campuses. A sample of attractive male and female students approached total strangers of the opposite sex and propositioned them, saying 'I find you very attractive' followed by one of three requests. These requests were (a) 'Would you go out with me tonight?' (b) 'Would you come over to my apartment tonight?' or (c) 'Will you go to bed with me tonight?' Clark and Hatfield found that while 50% of both men and women agreed to go out that night, none of the women propositioned agreed to sex with a total stranger and only 6% agreed to go back to their apartment later. However, a staggering 75% of men approached agreed to have sex – although only 69% of them agreed to go back to the person's house. Even when Clark modified the experiment in 1990 and assured participants about the trustworthiness of the stranger, the results were still the same – women did not generally agree to casual sex. The general unwillingness to engage in uncommitted sex is also found in lesbians (Buss and Schmidt, 1993).

Another difference in sexual behaviour relates to differences in sexual jealousy. While both men and women feel jealousy at betrayal by a partner, evidence shows that what makes them jealous may be different. Buss, Larsen, Westen and Semmelroth (1992) asked male and female students to imagine their current boy/girlfriend (a) having sex with someone else or (b) in love with them, and then asked which distressed them most. More women (85%) were distressed by emotional betrayal than sexual betrayal (15%). In contrast, more men were distressed by sexual infidelity (60%) than emotional infidelity (40%).

In an extension of the study, Buss and colleagues 'wired up' participants who were asked to imagine their partner having sex or in love with someone else, to measure various aspects of their stress responses including their heart rate, electrical activity of the skin and frown muscles. The researchers found that men became most physiologically aroused/distressed at the image of their partner being sexually unfaithful, whereas women became most distressed at the idea of their partner in love with someone else.

Thinking scientifically → **Ethics of research**

You may have noted that some of the studies carried out in this area have ethical implications. For example, Clark and Hatfield's studies on university campuses involved deception of participants and a lack of informed consent. This may also have led to feelings of stress when the students were propositioned by a stranger – or even disappointment as the students realized that the offer was not real! The study carried out by Buss and colleagues (1993) into sexual jealousy also involved a substantial degree of stress and emotional distress, even though participants consented to take part. Studies that ask people about their mate preferences avoid many of these ethical issues.

An important ethical principle of psychological research is the protection of participants with the aim of eliminating risks to their psychological well-being, physical health, personal values or dignity (BPS *Code of Ethics and Conduct*, p. 18). In studies of this nature, careful consideration of potential harm must be given before research can go ahead. Debriefing may also be used in studies that have involved a lack of consent.

Explaining these differences

Together, these studies have indicated that that there are some differences in the qualities sought by men and women in their partners (mate preference) as well as some differences in sexual tendencies and behaviours. We are now going to consider two explanations of these differences, which build on Darwin's ideas of sexual selection. The first of these is an influential explanation, which was put forward by Robert Trivers in 1972 and called parental investment theory (PIT). The second of these, sexual strategies theory (Buss and Schmidt, 1993), has built on the basis of PIT but sees human sexual behaviour as rather more flexible and strategic than Trivers originally suggested. Both theories work from the premise that mating is a human universal and that worldwide, 90% of people find a mate and marry at some point in their lives.

Parental investment theory

Trivers argued that the differences in sexual preferences and mating behaviours between males and females had their origins in the different amount of parental investment made by males and females. Trivers defined parental investment as 'any investment by the parent in an individual offspring that increases the offspring's chance of surviving (and hence reproducing) at the cost of the parents' ability to invest in other offspring' (cited in Barrett, Dunbar and Lycett, 2002: 34). Parental investment can be divided into mating effort (the physical act of having sex) and parenting effort (the raising of resultant offspring). Trivers' central argument was that the sex who invested the most in offspring should be choosy and discriminating in their choice of partner (inter-sexual selection) and the sex who invested least should compete most vigorously with other members of the same sex (intra-sexual selection) for access to mates.

How does this apply to people? The human male's investment in his offspring starts with mating effort. Men have large amounts of sperm and retain their fertility throughout their lives, unlike women who cease to be fertile after the menopause. Men are also capable of many matings and the only limit on the number of offspring they can produce is the number of available female partners they can persuade to have sex with them. Each mating can take little in terms of time and energy. In fact, a man can make a baby in less time than he can make a cup of tea. The male's optimal reproductive strategy – notwithstanding moral considerations – would be to have as much sex as possible with as many fertile partners as he can find. His main criteria in choosing females should be to ensure that they are fertile. It seems to make little sense in evolutionary terms for men to stay around when a woman is pregnant and help to raise the resultant offspring. Hence, his investment in babies could potentially end as soon as they have been conceived.

In contrast, the human female's investment in offspring is substantial. The gamete she supplies (the ova) is around one hundred times larger than the sperm and she has a limited supply of one ovum per month with twin births being rare. The reproductive life of a human female is shorter, at around 30 years, limiting the total number of offspring she can produce. Following conception, the female's pre-natal investment is essential for the survival of the baby. She carries the growing foetus for around 40 weeks feeding it from her own supplies of nourishment, which uses thousands of calories. She then must give birth. In the hunter-gatherer past, she would then continue to invest in the baby by breastfeeding for several years after birth. If these investments are not made, the child would be extremely unlikely to survive. The female's investment in parental effort is substantial in comparison to the male's and her best chance of reproductive success it to ensure the survival of her few precious offspring. This may be more likely if she chooses to mate with a partner who will stay around, invest in rearing offspring and protect and provide for the family unit. The female's optimal reproductive strategy is therefore to be choosy in her choice of mate, and seek a committed partner.

According to Trivers' theory, men and women are biologically at loggerheads. In fact 'Reproductive success for the two sexes is best achieved by different patterns of behaviour' (Hollway, Cooper, Johnston and Stevens, 2007: 144). But it is important to note that these sexual styles, preferences and behaviours are not seen as deliberate or rational by evolutionary psychologists: instead they exist simply because they brought survival advantages in the past.

Evaluation of parental investment theory

Trivers' theory has been supported by a wide range of studies which have examined mating behaviour of different animals. In mammals, the female is usually the main investor and there are plenty of examples of male competition and female choosiness in the animal kingdom. However, role-reversed species are also supportive of Trivers' claims. The male Panamanian poison-arrow frog invests more in bringing up offspring than the female. Female frogs are large and aggressive and compete for males who are choosy, showing that it is not biological sex as such that leads to mating behaviour but indeed the degree of parental investment.

Parental investment theory helps us to understand some of the differences in sexual behaviours in people which we described earlier. The first of these is *mate preferences*. As a woman invests heavily in each child, she should seek a man who has good genes to father her children and who shows commitment to remaining in the relationship and helping her raise offspring. If the male also has material resources, her offspring will be more likely to survive. This helps to explain women's universal preference for men with material resources shown in Pawlowski's study and Buss's cross-cultural analysis. It may also explain why women seek older men as they generally have more resources than younger men. Women also value indications of commitment that suggest that a man is likely to stay around and help to raise offspring. In contrast, males make less parental investment: they will be more reproductively successful if they have multiple matings with young, fertile females. This helps us to understand why men seek younger women and why physical attractiveness is universally important to men: in women, attractiveness is strongly linked to youth and fertility.

Trivers' theory can help to explain Clark and Hatfield's 1989 findings that men are generally more likely to engage in short-term sexual relationships than women. As one-night stands require little investment in time and effort, they can be seen as positive to men as they increase reproductive success. In contrast, females are less likely to be attracted to one-night stands as they do not display commitment in helping to raise the offspring which may result. However, PIT ignores the obvious evidence that women do engage in short-term relationships. Women also have affairs and one-night-stands: not all mating is about long-term relationships. A weakness of Trivers' theory is in the relative rigidity of the behaviours it suggests. Buss's sexual strategies theory takes this in to account and proposes that human mating behaviour is much more flexible than Trivers thought.

Trivers' theory also tells us little about homosexual relationships, which are non-reproductive: for example, it struggles to explain the reluctance of lesbians to engage in short-term, uncommitted sex when the risk of reproduction is not a threat. It also struggles to explain the preference for younger partners shown in older gay men.

◉ Sexual strategies theory

Sexual strategies theory (SST) was developed as an extension of Trivers' theory by Buss and Schmidt (1993). It accepts the basic premise of PIT that men and women faced different mating problems over the course of evolutionary history. However, Buss argues that both men and women have short-term matings (one-night stands, flings and affairs) as well as long-term relationships – although men generally devote more time to these than women. According to this theory, human mating is strategic: Strategies are simply ways of reaching goals and solving problems in pursuit of the overall goal of reproductive success. According to Buss and Schmidt, 'people look for different types of mates to solve specific adaptive problems that their ancestors confronted during the course of human evolution' (1993: 205). SST therefore differentiates between the strategies that men and women use when pursuing a short-term mate (for example a one-night stand or date) and a long-term partner. Rather than all women seeking commitment all the time and all men seeking youth and sexual availability, SST argues that different strategies will come into play depending on the situation.

Short-term mating

Short-term mating brings fairly obvious advantages to males in terms of reproductive success: men who had short-term matings and/or extra relational sex stood a good chance of increasing their reproductive success by fathering more offspring. However, there are also costs. These include contracting a sexually transmitted disease and acquiring a poor reputation that would prevent other females from mating with them. The main problems males have to solve in selecting female short-term partners are assessing their availability (are they willing) and ensuring they are fertile.

Females can also benefit from short-term mating. On the positive side, a short-term fling can provide benefits, for example, as 'mate insurance' in case her permanent mate disappears. However, there are greater potential costs for females than males, notably in gaining a reputation as promiscuous. This would have been more serious in the past for females as it may have led to their being disfavoured by well-resourced or powerful males as long-term mates. According to SST, the female faces the problems of identifying which short-term mates would provide good genes for offspring and which could provide resources, should they become long-term mates in her life. Any fling for a female should involve a generous male, as a stingy one is unlikely to provide resources later to possible offspring. In fact, females 'use short-term mating as an assessment device for long-term mating' (Buss and Schmidt, 1993: 217) to check out if the male is suitable as a long-term mate.

Long-term mating

When selecting a long-term partner, both sexes need to assess potential candidates carefully. Males face the serious problem of paternity uncertainty: they cannot be sure offspring are theirs unless they can guarantee the faithfulness of the female partner. Investing in offspring of another man would spell disaster in evolutionary terms. It is of crucial importance that the female they select will have good parenting skills otherwise offspring from the relationship may not survive.

For females, it is important to identify a potential partner who will be able and willing to supply resources to offspring and to offer commitment and protection. As well as this, a long-term mate should be healthy and supply good genes to resultant offspring.

Sexual strategies theory argues that while we are 'hard wired' to find certain characteristics desirable because they are advantageous in evolutionary terms, 'socially based' characteristics such as an outgoing personality or shared interests are also desirable. People are seen as strategists, using their hand of playing cards to secure reproductive success.

Evaluation of sexual strategies theory

Like Trivers' parental investment theory, SST can offer an explanation for many of the observed differences in behaviours we have considered. For example, both theories can explain the observed differences in sexual jealousy noted in Buss and colleagues' 1992 study. Men are more likely to become distressed at sexual betrayal in a long-term mate as it means that they may end up investing in babies that are not theirs. In contrast, women are more distressed at emotional betrayal in long-term relationships, as this may lead their partner to remove his support and resources, which may threaten the survival of the woman's offspring. In another study, 75 men and 73 women were asked about the likelihood of having sex with someone they had known for different intervals of time ranging from five years to one hour. Men were likely to answer 'yes, definitely' for all the time intervals up to about one week and would only be inclined to answer 'no' when they had known the woman for less than an hour! In contrast, women claimed they were unlikely to have sex with a man they had known for less than three months. Again this is consistent with both explanations that women are less disposed to casual sex.

However, SST extends our understanding beyond PIT by examining the qualities sought by both sexes in short-term encounters and it acknowledges that both short- and long-term mating may aid reproductive success in men and women. SST makes a large number of predictions about the qualities sought by men and women in potential long- and short-term mates. In a thorough review of the area, Buss and Schmidt (1993) identified support for their predictions. While we have not time to cover all these studies here, the following are presented for you to consider:

- In one study, Buss looked at the qualities men and women sought in short-term mates and found that women put high value on generosity in short-term mates in line with the predictions of SST. They also revealed themselves as much more choosy than men about the quality of short-term mates: 42 men and 44 women were asked about how bothered they were if a potential short-term mate was already in a relationship. Men were only mildly concerned about this, but women were much more concerned if the man was already attached. In an extension of this study, the same sample rated their response to promiscuity in a potential short-term mate: women viewed this as much more undesirable than men. Together, these studies imply that women and men view short-term mating very differently. Women appear to use short-term mating to assess long-term relationship potential as the theory suggests. If a short-term mating was really short term, then it should not matter whether the intended person is already in a relationship or is promiscuous.

- A second study comparing men's preferences for short- and long-term mates found that top qualities for men in long-term partners were faithfulness and sexual loyalty as the SST predicts. However, cross-cultural research has only partially supported this claim. Buss's (1989) review of partner preferences in 37 different cultures, found that men valued chastity more than women in 23 out of the 37 cultures. In the remaining 14 there were no apparent differences between men and women, suggesting that preferences for chastity vary across cultures. One possible explanation of this is that men may only become concerned about faithfulness *after* they have formed the relationship so that a women's sexual history beforehand is seen as less important.

Thinking scientifically → **The use of questionnaires in evolutionary psychology**

Most of the studies reported here by Buss and Schmidt have used a similar methodological approach: this has involved asking samples of men and women to rate specific qualities of potential partners or mates. These methods are often referred to as 'pencil and paper' methods. This approach to collecting data has many advantages. Considerable amounts of data can be collected fairly rapidly and summarized to identify patterns, trends and differences. However, what people say they want in partners and what they are actually prepared to accept may be very different in real life. In fact, people are adept at providing what they believe to be the correct – rather than truthful – answers to questions of this nature (Barrett, Lycett and Dunbar, 2002). For example, when asked ' If the conditions were right, would you consider having sex with someone desirable, if you had known that person for 6 months, 3 months, 1 month, 1 week, 1 day, 1 hour?' men were just as likely to answer 'yes, definitely' for all the time intervals up to about 1 week whereas women claimed they were unlikely to have sex with a man they had known for time intervals of less than 3 months. This data would imply that women do not have one-night stands – which may not be completely true.

The issue of accuracy need not be too much of a problem if researchers ensure that they are aware of response bias. In fact, deception (or telling lies) may also be seen as an interesting phenomenon in evolutionary terms: to tell an untruth of this nature requires the ability to identify what the other person believes to be the 'correct response' and points to the important role played by culture. The ability to lie and deceive is part of the idea of Machiavellian Intelligence proposed by Tooby and Cosmides (1992).

⊙ How do these theories apply to celibacy and gay and lesbian relationships?

You may have noticed that the theories and studies we have considered in this chapter have assumed that all relationships pursue the overall goal of reproductive success – babies! However, some people choose to stay celibate (not have sex) and many relationships are formed between couples who stay childfree or between same-sex couples. Can evolutionary psychology contribute anything of worth to understanding these relationships?

The puzzle of non-procreative relationships has challenged evolutionary psychologists, who have identified a number of possible explanations. One explanation of celibacy is that most celibate individuals have siblings and choose to invest in their nephews and nieces, which may maintain the survival of their own genes. Perhaps the most obvious explanation of gay relationships is that people have the cognitive ability to make choices about partners and relationships rather than being driven by instincts. Therefore, people might choose to prioritize immediate rewards of sexual relationships over concerns of reproductive success. Alternatively, if homosexuality has some genetic basis (and there is ongoing debate about this), it may be that it is associated with greater reproductive success in other family members. Some evidence has supported this claim. Gay men are more likely than straight men to have older brothers (Blanchard and Bogaert, 1996) and the sisters of gay men have been found to be super-reproducers who have many more children than sisters of heterosexual men (Iemmola and Ciani, 2009). These findings may eventually help us to incorporate and understand gay relationships within an evolutionary framework.

⊙ Commentary on the evolutionary perspective

The evolutionary explanations we have considered so far have emphasized the importance of predispositions that are coded for in genes. The evolutionary perspective takes the view that differences in sexual behaviour can be at least partly explained by genetic differences that have been selected in the course of evolutionary history. One problem with this is that the findings of many of the studies in this area are also consistent with other explanations. For example, Clark and Hatfield (1989) found that 75% of men – but no women – would agree to sex with a stranger. This could also be explained by the role of culture, which creates and circulates ideas about masculine and feminine behaviour, for example that 'nice girls don't'. In western society, social norms tend to see men as hunters pursuing women as prey. Female choosiness can be explained by gender role socialization and the cultural double standard which sees casual sex as acceptable and even desirable for men but not for girls. Some theorists (for example Dunbar et al., 1999) have suggested that evolution may shape cultural practices so that behaviours that were reproductively less successful become enshrined in cultural ideas. In the next chapter we will move on to consider how relationships are formed and organized today.

Summary

- There are broad differences in sexual behaviours between men and women including the tendency to engage in one-night stands, patterns of sexual jealousy and the desire for greater numbers of partners
- These differences have been explained by Trivers' parental investment theory (1972) and Buss and Schmidt's sexual strategies theory (1993)
- Parental investment theory argues that women invest more than men in offspring, which drives their general choosiness and makes them seek commitment. Men are seen as generally promiscuous in this model
- Parental investment theory says little about short-term mating especially in women

- Sexual strategies theory argues that men and women use different strategies and look for different qualities when seeking short- and long-term partners
- Reproductive behaviour is seen as complex and flexible

Further reading

An excellent introduction to evolutionary psychology is provided in *Human Evolutionary Psychology* by Barrett, L., Dunbar, R. and Lycett, J. (2002, published by Palgrave Macmillan). Chapters 5, 6 and 7 provide detailed accounts of mate selection, reproductive behaviours and parental investment theories.

Chapter 3

The effects of early experience on relationships

👁 Introduction

The evolutionary perspective focuses on how interpersonal relationships may have been shaped by thousands of years of evolution. During this lengthy period, the processes of natural and sexual selection are thought to have shaped relationship preferences and behaviours we see today. These preferences and behaviours have been coded in genes as predispositions.

However, human behaviour is not solely influenced by genetic predispositions. Humans experience an extremely long period of childhood and have a remarkable capability for learning through their experiences. Therefore, it is reasonable to assume that the relationships we have with other people as we are growing up are also likely to influence how we behave, think and feel with partners and lovers. These different relationships and experiences, 'teach us different lessons about what to expect from close partners' (Smith and Mackie, 2000: 440). In this chapter we are going to consider how experiences in childhood and adolescence may shape the relationships we have as adults. **Attachment** theorists such as Bowlby argued that the early relationships with our primary caregivers provide the basis for later adult relationships – an idea termed the **continuity hypothesis**. According to attachment theory, young children develop an **internal working model** from their first relationships as well as a characteristic **attachment type**. These influence their later relationships by providing the child with beliefs about themselves, other people and relationships in general. In order to understand the claims of the continuity hypothesis, we will start by considering Bowlby's attachment theory before moving on to consider the role played by attachments in children's friendships and adult relationships.

This chapter will consider:
- Bowlby's attachment theory and the internal working model
- Individual differences in attachment types in infants
- Attachment types and dimensions in adult relationships
- Methods of measuring adult attachments including the adult attachment interview
- The stability of attachment types from childhood to adulthood
- The influence/role played by attachments in children's friendships and adult relationships

Bowlby's attachment theory

Bowlby (1969) argued that the child's first relationships are crucial in understanding their subsequent development. It is within the context of these relationships – usually within the family – that children learn about trust, love and intimacy as well as the mechanics of relating. Although Bowlby focused his original theory on the importance of childhood attachments, others have developed his ideas and applied them to understanding adult relationships. Subsequent researchers and theorists have stated that we can only understand adult interpersonal relationships fully if we take into account the attachments between young infants and the people who bring them up. Although Bowlby's ideas were initially seen as controversial, they are now widely accepted within developmental social psychology.

What are attachments? These can best be thought of as emotional bonds between two people. These bonds, although invisible, can be inferred from observing attachment behaviours. We can tell that babies are attached to their parents by observing the ways in which they use the parent figure as a 'safe base' from which to explore the environment. We can also see how they return to the parent figure when they are scared or worried. Attached babies orient their behaviour towards their parent figure, protest when separated from them and show joy when reunited with them. Most of these behaviours can also be seen in an 'attached' couple: when they are separated they are likely to miss their partner and show relief and joy on reunion.

Bowlby drew his ideas about the importance of attachments from several different sources making his theory eclectic in approach. Some of the most important influences on Bowlby's theory are outlined below.

The evolutionary basis of attachments

Bowlby argued that the attachment between an infant and parent was an evolved mechanism that had been produced through natural selection because it ensured the survival of the child. He argued that behaviours shown by babies – such as crying and smiling – encouraged the mother-figure or parent to look after the baby. Those babies whose instincts were weak or who did not possess such behaviours would have been less likely to survive. He argued that parents possessed instincts designed to protect their baby from harm and to nurture them to ensure they survived to maturity. Parents who did not protect or nurture their infants would be less likely to produce surviving offspring. This would mean that their genes would be less dominant in the gene pool and would be likely to die out.

Bowlby also drew on **ethology**, a branch of science in which the behaviour patterns of non-human animals are studied. He noted the research of Konrad Lorenz (1935) which had shown that young birds will attach rapidly to a mother figure (or indeed any other large moving object), a process which Lorenz called 'imprinting'. Bowlby also drew on the work carried out by Mary and Harry Harlow (1962) with young rhesus monkeys. The Harlows had demonstrated how baby monkeys deprived of a real mother, used the surrogate mother to provide comfort and security when they were afraid, a concept Bowlby developed into the idea of a **safe base**.

The psychodynamic base of Bowlby's theory

Bowlby was initially trained as a psychodynamic theorist and he absorbed many of these ideas into his theory. Freud had argued that the relation-ship between baby and mother would create a 'prototype' for later rela-tionships and later object relations theorists such as Melanie Klein (1926) built on this idea. Bowlby developed the idea of a prototype further, arguing that the first attachment between the baby and the parent provided the child with an internal working model (IWM) for their future relationships which acted like a template, showing the child what to expect in later relationships.

Internal working models

We are not concerned here with all the aspects of Bowlby's attachment theory, simply those that are important in understanding later relationships. Bowlby argued that babies have a biological, inbuilt drive to form an attachment with a mother-figure. This term was used by Bowlby to indicate that any person, not necessarily the biological mother, could theoretically provide such a relationship. Bowlby believed that the formation of an attachment was a biological process that ensured the survival of the infant. He argued that this first, important attachment enabled babies to build up an IWM of how relationships work in general terms. The idea of the IWM included three components:

- *A model of the self:* Bowlby argued that each infant would build up an idea of their self through their relationship with their mother-figure. This would include feelings of self-worth from the way the mother-figure treated them. Children whose parents were responsive to their emotional needs would be likely to grow up feeling that they were worthy of love and attention.
- *A model of the mother-figure:* Bowlby argued that the child would develop an idea of how much their mother-figure could be trusted or relied upon to meet their needs for comfort and security. Children of sensitive and responsive parents would be more likely to feel that other people could be relied on and trusted than those whose parents did not notice their needs or responded inconsistently.
- *A model of the relationship between the two:* the child would build up a general idea of how relationships work and how people ask for support and comfort from each other.

Bowlby argued that the formation of a healthy IWM was crucial for the child's mental health and the adult's later psychological adjustment. He believed that the IWM provided a template or blueprint that would shape and influence the child's friendships and later romantic relationships, an idea often referred to as the *continuity hypothesis.* We will examine the evidence for this claim after we have considered differences in attachments.

👁 Different kinds of attachment

Bowlby's ideas about attachment were taken further by Mary Ainsworth, a colleague who had worked with Bowlby at the Tavistock Clinic in London. Ainsworth and her colleagues explored the idea that young child have different kinds of attachments with their mother-figures depending on the behaviour of the mother. Using the **strange situation** methodology, Ainsworth, Bell and Staydon (1971) explored the behaviours of young infants and mothers in a laboratory designed to look like a playroom. A large sample of babies aged around one year old were exposed to a series of short, three-minute episodes. These episodes included mother and baby together in the playroom and the entry of a stranger who attempted to interact with the baby. Following this, the baby was left by their mother with the stranger then rejoined by her. After this, the baby was left briefly alone. During these episodes, the behaviour of the babies and mothers was filmed through a two-way mirror, enabling the team of researchers to observe their behaviour.

Ainsworth et al. found three distinct patterns of behaviour in the infants, which they referred to as different attachment types. The researchers classified these as Type A (**Insecure-avoidant**), Type B (**Secure attachment**) and Type C (**Insecure-ambivalent** sometimes referred to as *Resistant*). A brief description of these attachment types is shown in Table 3.1.

Ainsworth's research demonstrated how attachment behaviours vary in infants. Her explanation of these differences related to the behaviour of the mother-figure, notably their sensitivity in responding to their child. Ainsworth argued that mothers who did not notice or respond to their baby's demands would produce babies who initially tried to gain attention but gave up following rejection. These babies seemed to expect little of their mother and treated the stranger in a similarly offhand way. Ainsworth argued that this treatment had led them to feel that they were unworthy of love and attention. In contrast, mothers who were responsive to their baby's needs would produce infants who felt secure. They would expect their mother to respond to their needs and would view her as a safe base that could be returned to when the environment was stressful. They would also develop feelings of self-esteem and would feel worthy of love and attention. They would carry these feelings of trust and confidence over to other relationships. Mothers who were inconsistent in their responses, who sometimes responded to the infant but not always, would produce more anxious babies who were unsure of their parent's affection. They would lack confidence that the parent would be available and would feel less worthy of love and attention. They would have less confidence in relationships.

	Type A Avoidant	Type B Secure	Type C Ambivalent
Behaviours in the strange situation	These babies showed little distress when their mother left and did not seek comfort when she returned. They seemed to expect little from the mother-figure and treated her in a similar way to the stranger.	These babies were happy to play and explore when the mother was in the room. They became distressed when she left. They were wary of the stranger although they did accept some contact with them. They welcomed the mother back when she returned settling down to play again quickly.	These babies showed distress when the mother left and rejected the stranger's attempts to comfort them. They did not settle down when the mother returned. They seemed unsure that she would come back and alternated their behaviour between approaching and avoiding the mother.
Model of the mother	These babies did not expect the mother to offer comfort or support and did not expect much from her.	These babies used the mother as a 'safe base' to explore. They seemed confident that they could return to her for comfort.	These babies seemed unsure how the mother would react and did not expect her to offer comfort consistently.

Table 3.1 The strange situation (Ainsworth, Bell and Staydon, 1971)

Since Ainsworth's original research, an additional attachment type has been identified by Main and Solomon (1990). Babies who did not appear to 'fit' within these three types have been categorized as Type D (disorganized or disoriented attachments). These infants show contradictory attachment behaviours cutting across the boundaries of Ainsworth's types.

Some critics have pointed to alternative explanations for these findings. The temperament hypothesis argues that a baby's responses do not come directly from the mother's behaviour but are largely inbuilt into the basic temperament of the infant. However, subsequent research has supported Ainsworth's claims: anxious attachment styles predominantly come from doubts that the attachment figure will be available (Cassidy and Berlin, 1994) and avoidant styles are adopted by infants who make unsuccessful attempts to gain closeness and proximity but are met with rejection or neglect (Simpson, Rholes and Nelligan, 1992).

Thinking scientifically → **The strange situation methodology**

Ainsworth's research has been criticized on both ethical and methodological grounds (Wood, Littleton and Oates, 2002). In the strange situation, babies were deliberately exposed to a range of stressful situations including separation from the mother-figure and contact with a stranger. All of these took place in an unfamiliar environment making it doubly bewildering for the infants. This was likely to be an unpleasant experience for many of the babies depending on their attachment type. However, Ainsworth's research allowed for the situation to be halted at any time by the mother or the researchers if a baby became very distressed.

A second criticism of the strange situation relates to its ecological validity. This study involved separation in an unfamiliar place. Critics have argued that this made it unlike real separations that take place in children's daily lives. For example, situations involving separation and care by babysitters generally take place in the familiar surroundings of the child's own home. Some have argued that the unreality of this very 'strange situation' means that this tells us little about real behaviour and attachment types because of this. However, it can also be argued that this situation does mirror many real life separations, for example when a child is left initially at nursery or playgroup, making the situation representative of real life.

Notwithstanding these criticisms, the strange situation methodology has been adapted by most people working with the field of infant attachments as the standard way of assessing attachment behaviour (Wood, Littleton and Oates, 2002).

Attachments in adult relationships: the Love Quiz study

Ainsworth's strange situation study demonstrated the existence of different kinds of attachment in young babies. In order to see if these attachment types applied to adults, a groundbreaking study generally known as the 'Love Quiz' was carried out by Hazan and Shaver (1987). The Love Quiz study set out to examine attachment styles in adults and to test the question 'Is love in adulthood directly related to childhood attachment type?' In order to collect their data, the researchers published a Love Quiz in their local North American paper, the *Rocky Mountain News*, and asked readers to write in and report different aspects of their relationship experiences. Respondents were asked to read the three descriptions shown in Table 3.2 (A, B and C) and then place a tick next to the alternative that best described how they felt in romantic relationships. They were advised that the terms 'close' and 'intimate' referred to psychological or emotional closeness, not necessarily sexual intimacy.

The second measurement used by Hazan and Shaver was a simple checklist of adjectives printed in the paper, which described their childhood relationship with their parents. Participants were asked to tick which items described the relationship as they remembered it (for example warm, fearful, detached). Respondents also completed a range of other questions including their beliefs about themselves, other people and relationships in general. Finally they were asked how long their different relationships had lasted.

Hazan and Shaver received over 1200 responses to their advert and selected 630 responses (215 men and 415 women) randomly from the readers who wrote in. They repeated this data collection exercise using a sample 108 university students with a mean age of 18 years providing a wide and varied pool of data. Hazan and Shaver's findings can be seen in Table 3.2.

Hazan and Shaver's study demonstrated the existence of Ainsworth's three main attachment styles – secure, avoidant and anxious – in adults. Of their first sample, 56% chose statement B, and were classed as securely attached (although subsequent studies such as Mickelson, Kessler and Shaver, 1997, have found this proportion to be slightly higher): this group were most likely to be happy and trusting of their partner and did not fear intimacy or closeness. They expressed a belief in lasting love, found others trustworthy and were confident that they were loveable. Around a quarter were classed as avoidant (respectively 23% and 25% in the two samples): this group were less accepting of their partners and were more doubtful about the existence of love in real life. They also felt that they did not need a happy relationship to get lots out of life. The final group were classed as anxious ambivalent: these people experienced the greatest feelings of jealousy and possessiveness and were often afraid of being abandoned. They fell in love easily and often but rarely found 'true love'. They felt insecure and experienced self-doubt in love.

Self-description	Attachment type	Beliefs about self, others and relationships
I am somewhat uncomfortable being close to others; I find it difficult to trust them completely; difficult to allow myself to depend on them. I am nervous when anyone gets too close, and often others want me to be more intimate than I feel comfortable being.	Type A Avoidant	I am not very easy to get to know It is rare to find someone you can fall in love with Romantic love rarely lasts
I find it relatively easy to get close to others and am comfortable depending on them and having them depend on me. I don't worry about being abandoned or about someone getting too close to me.	Type B Secure	I am likeable Other people are generally good hearted Romantic love can last
I find that others are reluctant to get as close as I would like. I often worry that my partner doesn't really love me or won't want to stay with me. I want to get very close to my partner and this sometimes scares people away.	Type C Anxious	I have many self-doubts I am not very easy to get to know Few people are willing to commit themselves to a relationship

Table 3.2 The Love Quiz (Hazan and Shaver, 1987)

Rethinking adult attachments: from types to dimensions

Hazan and Shaver's study demonstrated that the three basic attachment types appeared in adults in similar ways and proportions to those found by Ainsworth in young infants. However, the idea of measuring adult attachment using a 'single item' psychometric test was questioned by other researchers who noted that many people show characteristics of more than one of Hazan and Shaver's three categories, suggesting that they are not mutually exclusive. For this reason, attachment researchers began to devise multi-item questionnaires/inventories that measured many different aspects of attachment behaviours in close relationships. In order to simplify these, Brennan, Clark and Shaver (1998) used a statistical technique called **factor analysis** in which 323 questionnaire items in total were given to over 1100 students.

From their analysis, Brennan, Clark and Shaver (1998) identified the most important items that repeatedly came up as significant in distinguishing attachments. These 36 items related to two underlying dimensions, **anxiety** and **avoidance**. These dimensions are measured on a continuous scale (from high to low) with two opposing ends:

1 *Anxiety* – those scoring highly on the 'anxiety' dimension fear rejection and abandonment in close relationships. They experience distress when their partner is unavailable or unresponsive to them. They are likely to agree with items such as 'I resent it when my partner is away from me' and 'I get upset if my partner is not available when I need them'. Those with low anxiety are likely to agree to items such as 'I rarely worry about being abandoned'.

2 *Avoidance* – those scoring highly on the avoidance dimension fear depending on other people. They may be afraid of intimacy and have a strong need for self-reliance. They may also be reluctant to self-disclose personal information to partners. They are likely to agree with items such as 'I prefer not to show how I feel' and 'I try to avoid getting too close'. Those with low avoidance scores tend to agree to items such as 'I feel comfortable depending on my partner'.

The use of factor analysis has led to a new method of measuring adult attachments, the **Experiences in Close Relationships Scale** (ECRS) which is now extensively used. The ECRS consists of 36 statements chosen from the original 323 items. Of these, 18 relate to the anxiety dimension and a further 18 to the avoidance dimension. Some of the items are 'reverse scored', in order to prevent participants producing socially desirable answers. A shortened version of this scale has recently been produced by Wei, Russell, Mallinckrodt and Vogel (2007) and has been found to be both reliable and valid.

This research has enabled Brennan, Clark and Shaver to present a slightly different conception of adult attachments that incorporates and extends Ainsworth's original ideas about the three types. When placed together, these two scales divide attachments roughly into Ainsworth's three types, which are shown in Figure 3.1. Secure individuals obtain low scores on anxiety and avoidance. Those with an anxious preoccupied style score highly on anxiety but obtain low scores on avoidance. Avoidant individuals – not surprisingly – score highly on the avoidance scale. However, this group are further subdivided into those who score highly on anxiety (fearful avoidant) and those who are low in anxiety (classed as dismissing avoidant) thus extending Ainsworth's original ideas and presenting four attachment types. Brennan, Clark and Shaver's research demonstrates clearly how ideas and theories develop hand in hand with measuring tools.

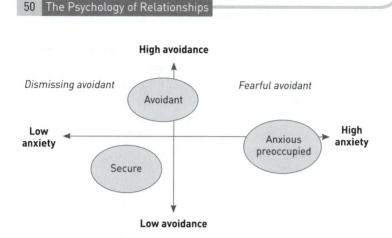

Figure 3.1 Adult attachment types (Brennan, Clark and Shaver, 1998)

Thinking scientifically → **Measuring adult attachment types (AAT)**

In this chapter you have met a variety of different methods of assessing adult attachments. While infant attachment types can be assessed using observational methods, these are not applicable to adults for several reasons. Firstly, adults must give consent if they are to be observed and they may alter their behaviour to show researchers what they want to see. Observing personal relationships is likely to be experienced as intrusive. When asked about relationships using self-report measures – such as the Love Quiz – adults are likely to compose answers that show the relationship or themselves in a favourable light, often referred to as a **social desirability** bias. This problem is further exacerbated by psychometric measurements that use single items (such as the Love Quiz) as these may overlap and be insufficient to distinguish between the different behaviours. When asked to recall memories of relationships with parents, these memories are likely to be 'fuzzy' and hard to describe.

For this reason, it has been necessary to devise alternative methods of assessing AATs that get around these problems. One such method is the **adult attachment interview** (AAI) devised by Main, Kaplan and Cassidy (1985). This looks at how the individual talks about their past rather than what is said. The AAI consists of a standardized interview in which a set of questions explore how adults describe the relationships they had with their parents to measure their current feelings about relationships. The focus of the analysis is not on the content of the interview but on the way the individual talks about their past relationships. The interview is coded by trained observers who look for a number of factors including the internal consistency (whether the individual makes contradictory statements) and coherence (if the points fit together). Using this method, Main and colleagues have identified three basic ways in which people talk about relationships with their parents:

1 *A dismissing narrative:* takes place where the person gives little detail and recalls events in a bland and unemotional way. They may also give the impression that the past is not very important.

2 *An autonomous narrative:* here the person talks about both the past and the present. The interview contains depth and detail of both positive and negative experiences.

3 *A preoccupied narrative:* in this narrative the individual talks in a rambling style without clear structure. Past events are often described with strong feeling or are dwelled upon. These feelings continue to seem strong in the present and the speaker may appear to be 'stuck' in events from the past.

The AAI is an extremely useful tool as it is relatively free from demand characteristics: while people may claim to have had a happy childhood, the coding of the interview may suggest that an adult could be classified as insecure from their narrative despite their claims. Since Main's original research, others have suggested that the overall interview can be transformed into a scale to give a 'Security Index' – a single score that provides some measure of overall security (Kobak et al., 1993).

Summary

- Attachments are emotional bonds between two people
- They have an evolutionary base and exist because they ensured the survival of infants in the past
- Bowlby argued that children use their first attachments to develop an internal working model, comprising ideas about themselves, others and relationships in general
- The strange situation showed how attachments vary in young children
- The Love Quiz demonstrated broadly similar attachment types in adults
- Adult attachments are more difficult to measure as self-report methods may produce socially desirable answers

- The adult attachment interview gets round this by examining how the narrative is constructed rather than what is said
- Adult attachment is now conceived of in terms of two dimensions, anxiety and avoidance, producing four broad types

👁 The influence of attachments on later relationships

As we noted earlier, Bowlby believed that early attachments were important in the child's adjustment and later relationships. In particular he argued that first attachments provide children with models or templates to deal with adult relationships, an idea often known as the continuity hypothesis. The continuity hypothesis makes two predictions about relationships:

1 Firstly, that internal working models persist from childhood to adulthood
2 Secondly, that internal working models have an effect on how people experience and conduct their later relationships.

What evidence is there for both of these claims?

Do attachment styles persist: continuity within limits

The best way to assess if attachment styles persist is to carry out longitudinal studies that examine attachment styles in the same group of people, starting in childhood and following them up into adolescence and adulthood. This is exactly what was done by Hamilton (1994). He studied a group of adolescents growing up in California and found a strong link between their childhood attachment type (CAT) assessed in infancy and their adult attachment type (AAT). However, Hamilton's study also demonstrated that attachment style could and did change in a few individuals. When major life events, such as divorce or bereavement, took place in children's lives, they could move from being classed as secure to insecure suggesting that there are limits to continuity. This idea has been confirmed by other studies, which have also found that life events and stressful experiences in childhood and adolescence may lead to insecurity in adult relationships. The Bielefeld longitudinal study carried out by Zimmerman et al. (2000) has examined the progress of a group of children growing up in Germany. Forty-four children were initially studied between 12 months and 18 months of age and classed using Ainsworth's attachment types. They were re-assessed for attachments to both mother and father at age 10 and again at age 16, using Main's adult attachment interview. This study found that child attachment type did not predict adult attachment type. Life events such as the divorce of parents or parental illness had much greater influence on later security.

Others studies have indicated that changes may occur in the other direction. Rutter, Quinton and Hill (1990) identified a group of people who had experienced problematic relationships with their parents but had gone on to achieve secure, stable and happy adult relationships which they termed **earned security.** Subsequent studies of earned secure individuals (for example Moller, McCarthy and Fouladi, 2002) have indicated that there are no significant differences in emotional responses to break-ups between those with permanent secure attachments and those with earned secure attachments, implying that later relationships and experiences can override early attachments. In support of this idea, Feeney and Noller (1992) have pointed out that relationship styles in adulthood vary: the same individual could be secure in a relationship with one partner but insecure in a later relationship, challenging the idea that attachment styles are consistent across different relationships.

These pieces of research indicate that early attachments may remain consistent if there are no major changes to 'derail' or dramatically alter attachment styles. However, they may also alter in response to experiences.

Attachment styles and children's relationships

The second claim of the continuity hypothesis is that that the internal working model provides a template for future relationships including friendships and romantic relationships. This idea suggests that we effectively take our experiences of trust and reliability of other people from childhood and transfer these to later friendships. Research has taken place to establish whether and how attachment types play a role in children's friendships with those of the same age, and later relationships. Most children grow up within a social environment surrounded by peers, friends and in many cases, siblings. Relationships with peers are characterized as **horizontal relationships** as they take place between two people of roughly equal knowledge and power. Peer relationships provide young people with the opportunity to develop and practise relationship skills and abilities. It would also be reasonable to assume that there may be a link between security of parent – child attachments and the quality of peer relationships.

The continuity hypothesis predicts that the child's attachment type/orientation are likely to exert an influence on friendships and popularity. The child who has a secure attachment style should be more confident in interactions with friends. Considerable evidence has supported this view. Waters, Wippman and Sroufe (1979), Jacobson and Willie (1986) and Lieberman (1977) have all found that children classified as 'secure' go on to be more socially skilled in their friendships than both types of insecure children. In one longitudinal study, Kerns (1994) measured attachments between a group of children and their mothers and then studied their play: 37 children aged just less than four years were selected along with their current 'best friend'. When the children were almost five, Kerns observed them playing with their best friend (6 boy-boy pairs, 7 girl-girl pairs and 8 mixed-sex pairs) and used behavioural measures to assess their play. She found that pairs of children who were both securely attached showed more positive play and adjusted their play to 'fit together' better. In support, Hartup (1989) has found that children with a secure attachment type are more popular at nursery and engage more in social interactions with other children.

What about children with insecure childhood attachment types? Lyons-Ruth, Alpern and Repacholi (1993) carried out a longitudinal study examining the school experiences of children classified using the strange situation methodology: 62 children from low-income families were assessed for attachment type at age 18 months and studied in the school environment at age 5. Lyons-Ruth et al. found that the strongest predictor of poor relationships at school was Type D (disorganized) attachment classification. Almost three-quarters of the children who were hostile or aggressive to other children had been assessed as having Type D attachment. These children seemed to struggle most to make friends with their peers. Insecurely attached children also tend to be more reliant on teachers for interaction and emotional support (Sroufe and Fleeson, 1986).

These studies support the claim that secure attachments with parents 'set up' children to be good at later friendships. However, there is a different explanation for these findings than that proposed by attachment theory. Russell and Finnie (1990) observed Australian pre-school children with their mothers in a situation where the child was introduced to unfamiliar peers. They found that mothers of children who were classed as 'popular' suggested strategies to help the child interact with other children and to 'ease' them into the group. They focused their help and instruction to their child on getting along with other children. In contrast, mothers of children classified as 'neglected' or unpopular focused their child's attention on object play. They encouraged their child to play with toys and materials but did not offer ways of helping them interact with other children. This study implies that popular children may simply be those whose caregivers model and teach important social skills. This explanation is consistent with the claims made by **social learning theory** which suggests that children learn relationship skills from parents via modelling – observation and imitation. Parke, MacDonald, Beitel and Bhaynagri (1988) argue that families indirectly influence their child's later relationships as they guide and modify the child's social behaviour to help them develop social skills.

Attachment styles and romantic relationships

As young people develop into adolescents, time spent with parents and family decreases and time spent with peers increases. At this age, friendships become increasingly intimate with higher levels of self-disclosure of inner feelings and secrets. Bee (1995) argues that teenagers use their peer group to make the transition from the protected place within the family to the wider adult world. Kobak et al. (1993) examined how attachment style influences adolescents' relationships with their parents. They found that those classed as secure showed less anger and more constructive behaviours when discussing a problem than insecure teenagers who were more likely to avoid the issue.

Attachment styles may also influence when young people start sexual relationships and how they organize and conduct these. Moore (1997) carried out a study using 100 adolescents aged 14/15 along with their parents and friends. She measured their attachment style using the AAI and asked a close friend of each teenager to rate their behaviour for social acceptability. Moore found that those classed as secure teenagers were less likely to engage in risky sexual activities (that is, unsafe sex) leading to pregnancy or sexually transmitted infections than their insecure counterparts. However, those classed as secure on the AAI were more likely to have had sexual relationships at this age than those rated as insecure. Moore concluded that secure attachments can help to 'set up' adolescents to handle the transition to adult sexual relationships.

Miller and Hoicowitz (2004) asked students to recall how long their different friendships and romantic relationships had lasted during their time at high school and to rate their attachments to parents. They found that a secure attachment to parents was the best predictor of adolescent relationships in length and quality, supporting Moore's claim that secure attachments 'set up' adolescents for romantic relationships.

William Hartup (1989) has argued that researchers know surprisingly little about the extent of cross-age linkages between attachments and later relationship experiences. This is for many different reasons: firstly, examinations of attachments are essentially a snapshot at a particular time, which may change because of stressors impinging on the parents. Secondly, children are likely to have a range of attachments, with parents, grandparents and other significant adults such as nursery or childcare workers, which will also influence their feelings of security. Outside events may also influence the nature of these relationships making it difficult to assess cause and effect in this area.

Attachments and adult relationships

Hazan and Shaver's (1987) study was one of the first to assess the continuity hypothesis by examining the link between CAT and AAT. As you will recall, their methodology involved asking their participants to select a series of adjectives that described the relationship with their parents as they remembered it. Hazan and Shaver found that childhood attachment was a good predictor of adult attachment. Secure Type Bs had relationships that had lasted on average twice as long as those classed as insecure. Similarly, Feeney and Noller (1992) examined the link between attachments and relationship breakdown. They studied 193 students and found that the three attachment styles differed: those with avoidant attachments were more likely to split up. However, they also found evidence for changes in attachment type when relationships changed from causal to committed, showing that attachment type is not completely fixed.

These studies have suggested that the attachment histories people bring to their relationships can provide some insights into how relationships are organized and conducted. We are going to end this chapter by looking at a couple of intriguing studies carried out by Jeffrey Simpson and colleagues to examine how attachments influence everyday relating between couples. In one study (Simpson, Rholes and Nelligan, 1992), dating couples were asked to take part in a piece of research in which they arrived together for an experiment. They were asked to wait separately and a state of high anxiety was created in the female members of each couple by showing them a room filled with alarming technological equipment. They were informed that the experiment involved high levels of stress (think of the ethics of this!) and then reunited with their partner to wait together for the next 'stage' of the experiment while the researchers observed them through two-way mirrors. The researchers found clear differences between those with secure and avoidant attachment styles in both use of their partners for support and the support offered.

Women who had previously been classed as securely attached were likely to share their anxieties with their partner and seek support and comfort. The women who had been classed as avoidant often did not mention their anxieties to their partner but kept them inside, giving them little chance to offer support even if it was needed. Men who were securely attached were likely to offer support to their partners based on the amount of fear they showed. The more upset the partner seemed to be, the more support they offered. However, avoidant men showed a very different pattern: the greater the fear or distress shown by the partner, the less support they offered. It seemed as if their partner's emotional neediness led them to withdraw from the situation.

In a second study, Simpson, Winterheld, Rholes and Orina (2007) recruited 93 heterosexual dating couples from a pool of university students, who had been going out together on average for 17 months (minimum length of relationship was 3 months). Simpson hypothesized that those individuals classed as secure via the AAI would be more likely to be calmed by emotional support and care whereas those classed as insecure would respond best to instrumental help such as practical or rational advice. Each member of the couple was initially asked to complete an AAI and then video-recorded while they discussed a current problem in their relationship. Observers rated and coded the interactions in terms of the kinds of support and caregiving offered. Simpson found the differences he had predicted between secure and avoidant participants. Secure individuals were most calmed by emotional support, while those who were avoidant reacted most favourably to offers of instrumental (practical) help and support. Simpson's ingenious studies – while unusual – give us a snapshot of how attachment styles might influence everyday relating and interactions.

Over the past ten years, a wealth of research has been published which has examined the role played by attachment style in many areas of relationship research. A considerable body of evidence has also accumulated relating to the importance of attachment styles in ways of dealing with relationship conflict. Those who are securely attached are more likely to act constructively when there is conflict by changing their own behaviour, whereas those who are less secure deal with conflict in less constructive ways (Levy and Davis, 1988). We will return to consider the role played by attachments in the formation, regulation and breakdown of relationships in the next three chapters.

⊙ Chapter summary

- The continuity hypothesis makes two predictions, that attachment type is relatively continuous from childhood to adulthood, and that attachment type influences later relationships
- There is limited support for the first claim. Longitudinal studies have shown that attachment styles only persist where major life events do not intervene. Events such as parental divorce and bereavement can lead securely attached children to become less secure in later life
- Insecurely attached children can gain 'earned security' through positive later relationships
- Many studies have demonstrated differences in friendships between secure and insecure children. Securely attached children tend to be more confident and popular with their peers
- Children with disorganized attachments have been associated with highest levels of hostility and difficulty in peer relationships
- Attachment style may also influence when young adolescents start sexual relationships and how safely they conduct them
- Studies of adults have suggested that those who are securely attached may have longer lasting relationships and provide more support for each other in stressful situations

👁 Further reading

Durkin, K. (1995) *Developmental Social Psychology.* Oxford: Blackwell. This text provides extensive coverage of attachments and peer relationships.

Smith, E.R. and Mackie, D.M. (2000) *Social Psychology.* Hove: Psychology Press. This text provides an excellent coverage of attachment styles and influences on adult relationships.

Chapter 4

Getting relationships started

Introduction

How do relationships start? In Chapter 2, we considered how sexual relationships may have been conducted in the distant past and how processes such as sexual selection may have shaped different relationship 'styles' and motivations for men and women. In this chapter, we will consider relationships in the twenty-first century. Relationships start in many different ways. Some people meet and fall in love; others get to know each other as friends before becoming romantically attached whereas still others meet in chat-rooms or via dating websites. We will start by examining some of the factors that influence whether or not two people are attracted to each other in these different environments. We will then move on to think about how and why initial attraction sometimes develops into a more serious relationship, by considering three theoretical models, Murstein's **matching hypothesis** (1972), Kerckhoff and Davis's **filter model** (1962) and **reward/need satisfaction theory**.

Most of the research studies and theoretical explanations covered in this chapter have been developed and carried out in western societies notably in North America and Northern Europe. These are often referred to as individualistic cultures: most individuals brought up in these countries share the belief that people are free to go out with different people, experiment with a variety of relationships and ultimately to choose their own partners. In western societies, relationships are seen as private arrangements between two individuals rather than alliances between families. As we have noted, many cultures do not share these views and favour different forms of arranged marriage. We will consider research into these relationships in Chapter 7.

In addition, many of the research studies and theories you will meet in this chapter have been based on heterosexual participants. The reason for this has largely been the level of social acceptance of same-sex relationships in the past. In the UK, homosexual relationships between men were illegal until 1967, which made them very difficult to study and largely 'invisible' to researchers. More recent types of relationships, such as those started and developed in cyberspace, have also been relatively understudied. We will consider some of the more recent insights into relationships formed via internet dating sites and between gay or lesbian couples.

This chapter will cover:
- Why we are attracted to some people rather than others
- The importance of physical attractiveness, similarity of background and attitudes in attraction
- Explanations of relationship formation including the matching hypothesis, filter model and reward/need theory
- Research into interdependence and commitment
- Dating and relationship formation via the internet
- Pathways to relationship development

Attraction

Boy meets girl, boy meets boy, girl meets girl. What will influence whether or not they are attracted to each other and begin the process of getting to know each other? As we noted in Chapter 1, the study of relationships focused almost exclusively on the processes involved in **interpersonal attraction** until the mid 1970s. This topic was appealing to social psychologists as it was relatively easy to study using the dominant research methods: experiments set in the laboratory and the field. From these early studies, researchers identified a range of factors that play a part in attraction. These factors included the importance of physical appearance, similarity of attitudes, interests and social background. However, in order for these factors to come into play, contact between two people is essential for any form of relationship to begin.

◉ Contact

Think for a moment about your current friends. It is likely that you have met many of them in the same handful of places: you may go to school, college or university together or work at the same place. You are likely to live fairly close to most of them. Until recently, most people met new friends and potential partners face to face. Relationships were most likely to be formed between people who lived near each other, who were placed in adjacent rooms in student halls of residence or who travelled on the same bus each day. In a classic study demonstrating this effect in 1932, Bossard found that more than half of 5000 couples applying for marriage licences in Philadelphia lived within a couple of minutes' walk from each other. In 1950, Festinger, Schachter and Back compared the friendships formed by students in halls of residence and found that people were far more likely to be friends with those who lived on the same floor or corridor than those from the floor above or below. Friendships with people on other floors were much more common in those who lived in the room next to the stairs. Living near someone or working at the same place allows regular and relatively easy contact and provides an opportunity for people to get to know each other.

Over the past twenty years, physical proximity has become a less important factor in attraction. Developments in communication technologies such as texting and internet use mean that it is possible to get to know someone with little or no face-to-face contact – think of the number of people who meet via an internet dating site or in a chat room. Despite this, regular contact – whether this is face to face or online – remains important because it allows two people to get to know each other. It is also important as it leads to an expectation of continued interaction: if we know we are going to be able to meet or chat again, this makes the possibility of a relationship real so it may be worth spending time getting to know someone.

◉ Physical appearance and attractiveness

When two people meet face to face, physical appearance generally plays a role in attraction. One of the first things we notice about other people is what they look like and how they present themselves physically in terms of clothes and hair. We considered in Chapter 2 (evolutionary psychology) which bodily features make men and women physically attractive and how these may relate to reproductive success in the past. How important are these factors in the twenty-first century? Common ideas about beauty suggest that it is of little importance in attraction. Think of the following sayings: 'Beauty is in the eye of the beholder', 'Never judge a book by its cover' and 'Beauty is only skin deep'. All of these imply that physical appearance does not matter and is not used as a basis to judge or evaluate another person.

Langlois et al. (2000) set out to test the three statements above by carrying out 11 *meta-analyses* of a total of 919 research studies that had examined physical attractiveness. They found that the first two sayings were contradicted by evidence. Firstly, there was considerable agreement within and between different cultures as to who was attractive and who was not. This suggests that there is a shared understanding of physical beauty, rather than beauty being defined individually. Secondly, Langlois et al. found that adults and children who were rated as good-looking were judged more positively by other people, and treated better if they behaved badly, showing that many people judge others on their appearance. The assumption that beautiful equals good is called the 'halo effect' and it may well be absorbed by young children from films and fairy stories, where good looks often go with a kind personality. However, Langlois et al. found evidence to contradict the third saying. Physically attractive children generally showed *more* positive behaviours and nicer personality traits than children who were deemed unattractive, suggesting, somewhat surprisingly, that beauty may be more than skin deep. Of course, it is possible that attractive children are treated more positively and this leads them to develop positive behaviours and pleasing personalities.

Is physical appearance of equal importance to everyone?

The simple answer to this is no! Some people put a greater emphasis on the appearance of their partner and value physical attractiveness more highly. Some of these differences relate to personality and others may well be broad differences based on sex. Snyder, Berscheid and Glick (1985) found that high self-monitors (people who are acutely aware of how they appear to others and who care strongly about acting in a socially approved way) placed a higher value on the physical appearance of a potential partner than low self-monitors who were more concerned about the personality traits of their partner than their looks. Physical appearance generally seems to be more important to men than to women. This was demonstrated in studies using personal column adverts (Dunbar and Waynforth, 1995), which showed that physical attractiveness was sought by 44% of men compared with 22% of women. Cross-cultural studies (for example Buss, 1989) have demonstrated that this finding is robust across all cultures and it also applies regardless of sexuality: gay men are more concerned than lesbians with the appearance of their partner, as we will see later in this chapter.

⊙ Similarity of attitudes and personality

Once two people have started talking to each other – either face to face or using texts or the internet – their interests and attitudes become important. The importance of attitude similarity in attraction received considerable research in the 1970s and culminated in the **law of attraction** proposed by the psychologist Don Byrne (1971). The law of attraction simply states that the closer someone shares our attitudes, the more we will like them. Byrne tested this idea using the **Bogus** (pretend) **stranger** technique. Participants, who believed they were waiting to take part in another experiment, were asked to fill in questionnaires about their attitudes to many different topics. The researcher then took their questionnaire and rapidly constructed a profile of another individual (the Bogus stranger) systematically varying the degree of attitude similarity to the real participants. When presented with details of this 'stranger' and asked how much they would like to meet them, Byrne found that the amount of attraction and liking related strongly to similarity – the closer the two sets of attitudes, the more participants thought they would like the person.

Studies of this nature have been widely criticized for lacking validity. In the case of Byrne's research, the *only* information participants had to judge the stranger was their attitudes. In real life, it would be unlikely that two people would find out so much about another person's attitudes on a first face-to-face meeting. They would also have other kinds of information to base their judgements of attraction on – notably physical appearance. In fact, a meta-analysis of 313 studies of attraction using both laboratory and field settings (Montoya, Horton and

Kirchner, 2008) has suggested that attitude similarity leads to attraction only in 'no interaction' situations like Byrne's or in short-term interactions with strangers. In field studies using real relationships, similarity of general attitudes appears much less important than initially thought by Byrne.

Byrne clearly overestimated the importance of shared attitudes. However, there is no doubt that similarity plays a role in attraction. Communication is easier when two people share attitudes and shared interests are also important as spending time together is easy and rewarding. One area where attitude similarity does seem to be important is in attitudes towards sex: we are likely to form relationships with people who share our attitudes toward sex (Cupach and Metts, 1995) and this similarity is even more marked in lesbian and gay couples. Conversely, differences in attitudes can certainly lead us to dislike people (Singh and Ho, 2000).

A related issue is whether real similarity is important in the development of relationships or whether perceived similarity is more relevant. If we think someone is quite like us (even if they are not), this may lead us to want to get to know them more. In order to test this claim, Selfhout, Denissen, Branje and Meeus (2009) studied the process of friendship formation and attraction in a much more realistic situation when first year students (known as 'freshers') start at university. A group of 378 first year students in the Netherlands (average age 18.9) were asked to complete an online personality questionnaire rating themselves using the **Big Five Personality Inventory**. They were then asked to assess the personalities of other students in their tutor groups. After several months, they were asked to rate their liking for their classmates using a scale of 1 (hardly know the person) to 7 (best friend). This allowed the researchers to assess the effects of actual similarity (measured by the closeness between two students' completed personality profiles) and perceived similarity (measured by the closeness between the student's rating of their own personality and their rating of the other person's).

If you have followed this so far, you may want to know what happened. Selfhout et al. found that actual similarity between two people was not very important in relation to liking. However, perceived similarity correlated strongly with higher liking. If a student saw themselves as being like another person, they were likely to like them and be attracted to them – even if, in reality, they were pretty different!

Thinking scientifically → **Different ways of doing social psychology, then and now!**

These two studies provide a very good opportunity to examine how research into attraction has changed and developed over the past forty years. As we noted in Chapter 1, Byrne's study was typical of many social psychology experiments of the 1960s and 70s. The study was carried out under laboratory settings and characterized by high control. In order to manipulate attitude similarity (the independent variable), Byrne created the profiles of strangers himself so that he could vary precisely the degree of shared attitudes. Participants were asked to rate the 'stranger' once (the dependent variable) and there was no follow-up to assess how the relationship had developed, as the stranger did not really exist. The assumption was that outside factors, previous relationships, mood and current state simply had no effect on the dependent variable.

Compare this to the 2009 study. In this, real people in a real life, high-stakes setting (the start of a university year) were asked to carry out personality tests in an online format. This was likely to lead to lower levels of demand characteristics and higher levels of honesty. Measurement of their personalities used the Big Five personality test, which is a well-validated tool. The students were then reassessed over a period of several months as they developed natural friendships within the group. Rather than a single snapshot, this longitudinal study enabled the researchers to see how friendship patterns and relationships developed over a period of time. Researcher manipulation in this study was minimal – they simply attempted to capture what had happened and looked for explanations of these patterns.

Demographic similarity

Another area of research has found that demographic similarity is important in both platonic friendships and in attraction. We are most likely to become friends and form romantic relationships with people who are a similar age to us, who come from a similar socioeconomic class, social background and ethnic group. This is partially explained by contact: we are most likely to meet, go to school and work with people who live near us and are similar in various ways. Kandel (1978) found that teenage pairs of close friends were similar in many respects including ethnic background, religion and economic background of parents. Hill, Rubin and Peplau (1976) also found similarity of race, class and religion in dating couples and in pairs of friends.

Liu, Campbell and Condie (1995) have looked at similarity of ethnic background in a sample of American students. Students from four ethnic groups – Asian, African, Latino and White – were asked about their preferences for dating partners. All chose their own ethnic group as most desirable over potential partners from other groups even though they sometimes rated another group as more physically attractive. When asked about the reasons for choices, the most common answers related to social networks: potential partners from their own ethnic background were more likely to be approved of and welcomed by family and friends. We shall return to this later, in Chapter 7.

As we noted in Chapter 2, age was important in mate choice in the past and continues to be important in attraction today. Greater reproductive success was achieved by men who chose to mate with younger, fertile women and by women who chose older men who were prepared to input time and resources into raising offspring. If you look around your friends today, it is likely that you will find that most dating relationships have an age gap, with girls choosing to go out with boys who are two or three years older than themselves. Dunbar and Waynforth (1995) analysed 900 personal column adverts and found that a younger partner was important to just under half of men (42%) compared to a quarter of women.

◉ How important are these factors in attraction and relationship formation?

Sprecher (1998) carried out research using a sample of 381 students (mean age 20.3) to examine how important they perceived different factors were in attracting them to their current partner. 'Attached' participants who were going out with someone were asked to rate the importance of a range of factors to their current relationship. Sprecher found that four factors were consistently rated as important to attraction: warmth and kindness, having a desirable personality, reciprocal liking and something unique or specific about the other person. These qualities were – interestingly – pretty much the same as those that people valued in their friends! There was little mention of the importance of physical appearance or similarity! This demonstrates an important principle which we considered in the last chapter: what people do/value and what people say they do using pencil and paper measurements can often yield different sets of data as many people will provide socially desirable answers when asked about their views of relationships.

⦿ Understudied relationships: same-sex relationships

Until fairly recently, people who were same-sex attracted found it more difficult to meet potential partners, as it was hard to identify others who might be gay or lesbian. This meant that young gay men and lesbians tended to be later in starting relationships, often waiting until they left home. However, in western societies, the increasing acceptability of same-sex relationships, along with venues like gay bars and clubs, has made it easier for people to meet and identify potential same-sex partners. An Australian study carried out by Hillier and Mitchell (2008) found that young same-sex attracted people became sexually active earlier than heterosexual teenagers often through the desire to check out their sexuality and 'settle the matter' of who they were attracted to. However, gay couples still face considerable discrimination and prejudice. Simple behaviours taken for granted by many heterosexuals, such as holding hands and showing affection in public, may lead to verbal abuse. Same-sex relationships exist within an inhospitable social climate (Kurdek, 2005), as we will explore further in Chapter 5.

A range of studies have examined the preferences of gay men and lesbians in terms of attractive qualities sought in partners. Personal column adverts of gay men and lesbians (Deaux and Hanna, 1984) show a similar story to those of heterosexual people: gay men are more likely to request physical attractiveness in a partner than lesbians. Bailey and Zucker (1995) have compared the preferences of gay and straight men advertising for partners and found them to be very similar. Both showed a high interest in the physical attractiveness of their partner and were relatively uninterested in the financial status of potential partners.

Similar age 'rules' appear to apply to gay relationships: Kenrick et al. (1995) compared the age preferences of gay and straight men. Using 783 singles adverts taken from a range of New York magazines, they found strikingly similar preferences. Both groups of men were happy with the idea of a partner who was up to five years older or younger when they were in their twenties. However, as both groups aged, their preferences moved gradually towards younger partners, which continued across adulthood.

⊙ Getting to know you in cyberspace: the attractions of online relationships

Many relationships begin in chat rooms or on internet dating sites, before moving to a face-to-face format. Over the past ten years, social interaction has become the most important use of home computers (Kraut et al., 2000) and the growth of internet dating sites has been remarkable. Early models of computer mediated communication (CMC) were divided as to whether it led to losses of important social information such as facial expressions and non-verbal behaviours (for example reduced cues theory) or to gains. Walther's 1996 'Hyper-personal communication model' is in the 'gains' camp and suggests that online interaction is more social (that is, lets us pass one more information) than face-to-face interaction because people can 'optimize their self presentation' (Joinson and Littleton, 2002: 340). Or, to put it simply, the internet gives us more control over the impression others form of us, making it an attractive arena to meet and get to know people. Why is this?

1 Firstly, on many internet dating sites, the format of CMC is asynchronous, meaning that people do not talk in 'real time' but post messages which are read at a later date. This means that people can spend more time composing and editing messages to present them in the best light. This is also true of instant messaging (IM) although to a lesser extent: even here, people have more time to think about their responses than in a face-to-face setting.

2 Secondly, people are unable to 'see' each other (except in the form of a carefully chosen photo placed on a profile or through a webcam). This can mean that physical appearance becomes less important in the early stages of getting to know someone. When people are freed from concerns about their appearance, they can become more open about their feelings and thoughts.

The above points suggest that CMC could enable individuals to create and develop positive impressions of themselves. On the other hand, these could be very misleading, with daters claiming they are older, younger, richer or more attractive than reality. What does research tell us about the formation and development of online relationships?

Who uses dating sites?

One strand of research has attempted to establish who uses dating sites along with the reasons or motivations for choice. Lawson and Leck (2006) studied the motivations of a group of internet daters, focusing on their reasons for choice of internet dating, the styles of courtship used on sites and how they dealt with the thorny areas of trust (believing what people tell you) and deception (being truthful). Lawson and Leck's participants gave a number of reasons for their choice of internet dating: some were seeking companionship and others sought comfort after an emotional crisis such as divorce or bereavement. Participants believed that internet dating provided them with a great deal more freedom in relationships than face-to-face dating: firstly, freedom over the impression they formed and the ways in which they presented themselves and secondly, freedom from traditional, stereotypical dates scenarios.

Another advantage of online dating is the ease of developing several relationships at the same time. Detter (2006) compared traditional and online daters in terms of how much attention they paid to romantic alternatives and found that those with a history of internet dating kept more of an eye on other relationship possibilities than traditional daters. These studies support Walther's claims of gains in the online dating environment and imply that internet dating may well be attractive as it frees people up from traditional face-to-face pressures and norms.

How do people present themselves on dating sites?

Whitty (2008) examined the internet profiles placed by 30 men and 30 women on dating sites. She also interviewed each participant and asked them how they constructed their own profile, why they chose to include certain kinds of information and what they looked for in other people's profiles. Whitty found that people choose to present themselves in deliberate and strategic ways to create specific impressions. She also concluded that the main differences between internet dating sites and other forms of dating were the sheer amount of information available and the depth and breadth of self-disclosure before two people held a one-to-one conversation. Many studies (for example Joinson, 2001) have confirmed that people disclose more personal information about themselves at a much faster speed in a CM environment than face to face.

> ### Thinking scientifically → **Research study: 'Taking Goffman on a Tour of Facebook'** (Birnbaum, 2009)
>
> One phenomenon that can hardly have escaped you in the past decade has been the growth of social networking sites such as Facebook, MySpace and Bebo. Unlike most other internet sites, these are unique in that people tend to meet face to face first, and are then added as friends showing an offline to online trend.
>
> Birnbaum (2009) has carried out an interesting study examining Facebook pages of students to consider how they create a picture or profile of themselves. He used a combination of methods including participant observation (as a Facebook member), 30 interviews and a content analysis of the photos posted on pages. Birnbaum found that students used a fairly small number of ways of presenting themselves, which he called 'fronts' after the work of Goffman (1956). The main ' fronts' included the party/social animal, showing the person in a group of friends, the risk taker/adventurer engaging in daring activities and the comic/humorous figure having a laugh. Other images/ strategies involved presenting the self as a member of the larger community group and as unique.
>
> Profiles on Facebook are clearly designed to create a particular image or an impression for those who know us – and those who would like to get to know us better. Birnbaum argues that these different 'fronts' make up a picture of the ideal student: popular, surrounded by friends, having a laugh, which should create favourable impressions in people visiting their page.

Together these studies imply that internet sites allow people to feel much more in control of the ways in which they present themselves and the impression they can create in potential partners. This also has the function of freeing them from forms of dating that may be constraining. But what happens when relationships move from online format to face to face? As yet, this has received little by way of systematic investigation.

Summary

- Contact, physical appearance and similarity are important in attraction

- Contact provides opportunities for two people to meet, face to face or online
- Physical attractiveness is generally found to be more important to high self-monitors and to men
- The 'law of attraction' overrated the importance of attitude similarity. Perceptions of similarity may be more important than actual similarity
- Similarity of age, ethnic background and education is also important in attraction
- Similar factors are important in same-sex relationships
- Online dating is becoming increasingly popular. Asynchronous messaging provides more time for positive self-presentation and freedom from concerns about appearance
- Self-disclosure of beliefs, feelings and attitudes occurs more rapidly in online relationships than face to face
- Online daters value the freedom from traditional dating concerns and the option of developing several relationships simultaneously

◉ From attraction to relationships

Once two people have met and begun to get to know each other, how likely is it that this will develop into a longer-term relationship? Lots of relationships fail to get off the ground or simply fizzle out. There are many reasons why two people may not pursue a relationship with each other even when there is strong attraction: they may be involved with someone else, wary from a previous split or decide that the relationship is not viable due to practical reasons such as moving away to university or living too far apart. Alternatively, they may face opposition from family or friends who disapprove of their partner. It could also be that the relationship may appear to work for a period of time but may fizzle out at a later date as it fails to meet the partners' needs or their circumstances change.

Here we will consider three theories that attempt to explain how and why relationships between two 'attracted' people might develop.

The matching hypothesis

An early explanation of attraction and relationship formation was proposed in the 1960s and called the 'matching hypothesis'. This hypothesis originally made two predictions:

1   The more socially desirable an individual is, the more socially desirable they would expect their dating partner to be. Social desirability can include how good-looking, clever or indeed rich the person is.

2   Couples who are matched in social desirability will be happier and more likely to stay together than those who are mismatched.

The matching hypothesis was tested with a range of studies using 'blind dates' which involved pairing two strangers together and seeing if they wanted to see each other again (for example 'The computer dance study' – Walster, Aronson, Abrahams and Rottman, 1966). Most of these studies gave little support to the matching hypothesis and showed pretty much the opposite of what was predicted: that 'everyone likes a socially desirable person, regardless of his or her own level of social desirability' (Sprecher, 1998: 35).

However, later studies in much more realistic surroundings provided some support for the idea of matching in relation to physical attractiveness. Murstein (1972) took photos of 99 couples who were dating and asked a sample of participants to rate each member of the couple for attractiveness. He then compared these ratings with photos of men and women who were randomly paired into couples. Murstein found that the real couples were consistently rated as more alike in levels of attractiveness, supporting the first claim of the matching hypothesis. People were matched with someone who was broadly similar to themselves in level of attractiveness. Similarly, Silverman (1971) supported the hypothesis by surreptitiously rating couples in bars and restaurants and again finding them to be roughly matched in their levels of physical attractiveness. Murstein explained these findings by suggesting that, while we might desire the most physically attractive partner in theory, in reality we know that we are unlikely to get or keep them so we look for someone of a similar level of attractiveness as this makes us less likely to suffer rejection. Studies have also suggested that the 'matching' concept can also be applied to pairs of friends. McKillip and Riedel (1983) found that pairs of school friends were also fairly closely matched in levels of physical attractiveness.

The matching hypothesis is a useful way to consider how people 'sort' themselves into early relationships. However, it is quite apparent that many couples are 'mismatched' in levels of physical appearance. This is probably because social desirability relies on many more factors than appearance: intelligence, personality and wealth can also make someone socially desirable, suggesting that matching is multifaceted and complex. In many countries where women earn less than men, young attractive women may 'trade off' their appearance to enter a relationship with a man who possesses wealth and resources but who is not physically attractive (Waynforth, 2001). Sprecher argues that the matching hypothesis helps us to understand why two people might choose to go out with each other initially but **social exchange** approaches such as **equity theory** help us to understand why the relationship develops from initial attraction to longer term. We shall consider what exchange theories have to tell us about relationship development in the next chapter.

Kerckhoff and Davis's filter model (1962)

The filter model also considers how initial attraction develops into a longer-term relationship. This rather elegant little theory argues that the factors we considered earlier (contact, age, similarity) become important at different times in a developing relationship. Different factors or criteria are used as filters at different times, so that the large field of potential partners (called the **field of availables**) is gradually narrowed down to a relatively small group from whom we select our partners (the **field of desirables**). The filter theory suggests that we 'filter out' many people as 'unsuitable' and narrow down to a relatively small group of people who we would consider as potential partners:

1   According to the filter model, the first filter involves social/
    demographic variables such as age, similarity of social background
    and social class. Kerckhoff and Davis argued that this filter exerts
    its influence without our being aware of it most of the time. Most
    people tend to meet other people who are pretty similar to them in
    key ways – who are the same age, live in the same area, who go to
    school, or university with them or who work at the same place.
    Other people who live in different areas, who go to different schools
    or have left school and started work, are less frequently

encountered. This provides a fairly small selection of people who are often similar to us. This is the first 'field' from which most of our potential partners are chosen.

2 Once two people have started getting to know each other, the second filter is similarity of attitudes and values. When two people share interests, attitudes and beliefs, communication is usually easier and the relationship may progress. If, however, they appear to be very different, to have little in common and few shared interests, it is likely that a relationship may not progress. At this stage, people with different interests, attitudes and values are filtered out. We may go out with them a few times, but the relationship peters out or fails to take off. People who get through this second filter are those who we have something in common with and who we can talk to and share activities with.

3 Once two people have become established in a relationship and have started to get to know each other fairly well, the third filter comes into play. This is complementarity of emotional needs between the two people – how well the two people fit together as a couple and meet each other's needs. For example, a relationship in which one person wishes to settle down but the other does not may founder at this stage, when the two people involved have very different needs from the relationship.

Kerckhoff and Davis's model encompasses many of the factors we have considered so far and suggests when they may be most important. A considerable amount of evidence supports the claim that demographic similarity and attitudes are important in relationship development. Sprecher (1998) found that couples who were matched in physical attractiveness, social background and interests were more likely to develop a long-term relationship. A longitudinal study of couples over 21 years found that those who were similar in educational level and age at the start of their relationship were more likely to stay together. They also became more similar in attitudes as time went on (Gruber-Baldini, Schaie and Willis, 1995).

Kerckhoff and Davis (1962) tested their model using a longitudinal study of student couples who had been together for more or less than 18 months. They were asked to complete several questionnaires over a seven-month period in which they reported on attitude similarity and personality traits with their partner. In line with the predictions of the filter model, it was found that attitude similarity was the most important factor up to about 18 months into a relationship. After this time, psychological compatibility and the ability to meet each other's needs became important, demonstrating that different factors may be important at one time but may assume less relevance later on.

Reward/need satisfaction theory

Our third explanation of relationship formation focuses on why relationships are formed between some people and not others. In order for a relationship to progress from early attraction, the two people involved need to be sufficiently motivated to want to continue getting to know each other. Reward/need satisfaction theory argues that a long-term relationship is more likely to be formed if it provides rewards or 'reinforcements' or at least promises rewards in the future! Foa and Foa (1974 cited in Sprecher, 1998) identified six types of rewards that could be gained from a relationship including status (being someone's girlfriend or boyfriend), love, money or financial support, goods and services and information. Less savoury rewards could include the satisfaction gained from showing a previous love interest that we have 'moved on'. There are also more obvious rewards of enjoying shared activities and time spent together. Allied to this model is the idea of classical conditioning which argues that we are more likely to be attracted to someone if we associate them with rewards

People enter relationships with a range of needs and the relative strength of these varies between individuals. Some of these include the need for affiliation, the need to feel good about yourself (self-esteem), the need to be nurtured or looked after (dependency) and needs for power and dominance over others. If the rewards offered by one person meet the needs of the other, this is likely to motivate them to develop the relationship further. So for example, when someone shows they like you, this can be rewarding and feed your need for self-esteem, making you feel good about yourself. When your partner comforts and hugs you after a bad day, this meets your dependency needs. Evidence shows that the meeting of needs is an important factor in the long-term survival of relationships. Smith and Mackie (2000: 463) argue that long-term, happy relationships meet many of the needs of the two people involved whereas unhappy relationships involve unmet needs.

It seems obvious that a relationship is more likely to get off the ground if the two people enjoy time spent together, find each other's company rewarding and meet each other's needs. Early attempts to test this theory involved rather contrived laboratory experiments in which strangers met each other in different environments, rewards were manipulated and their attraction to each other was measured. For example, Veitch and Griffith (1976) arranged for pairs of strangers to watch a TV programme while 'waiting to take part in an experiment'. Some of the programmes showed a 'feel good' news bulletin whereas others focused on gloomy news. When asked how much they liked the other person, those in the happy news condition rated them as more likeable and attractive than those in the gloomy condition, supporting the idea that we can associate rewards with other people.

Studies of this nature have been roundly criticized for their artificiality and the inability to generalize their findings to everyday, real life situations. However, rewards are clearly important in determining how a relationship will develop (Rusbult and van Lange, 1996). Clark and Mills (1979) identified two distinct ways in which couples exchanged rewards: on a 'tit for tat' basis (I will cook for you tomorrow if you cook for me on Thursday) and in a less reciprocal way where rewards are given without thought of paying back out of a desire to please the partner. They called these **exchange relationships** and **communal relationships**. The move from giving rewards on an exchange to a communal basis may be an important aspect in forming a close relationship.

Comparing these theories

All three theories agree that longer-term relationships are most likely to be formed where partners meet each other's needs although they take different views of when different kinds of needs become important. They address the issue of relationship formation in different ways and take different levels of analysis. Reward theory takes an experimental social approach to relationships by assuming that people think about their relationships, weighing up ideas about rewards. It looks at individual needs and rewards as motivations for relationship formation and considers people to be basically selfish – a view shared by the **economic approaches** we will cover in Chapter 5.

Both the matching hypothesis and the filter model see relationships as existing within a framework in which social and cultural factors are important. The matching hypothesis takes the view that social factors are important by suggesting that we take on board ideas about our own worth and other people's value in seeking a 'matched' partner. In the filter model, the demographic filter suggests that social sorting – where we live, our level of education and our age – influence who we get to meet and who we see as potential 'relationship material'. However, most of the research used to 'build' this model was carried out on relationships where attraction and relationship formation takes place face to face. The rapid expansion of communication technologies over the past two decades has allowed people to get to know each other using the internet and mobile phones. This allows us to interact with a much wider field of people than those who live and work locally and suggests that the social/demographic filter proposed by the filter model may be much less important in relationship development.

◉ The developing relationship: commitment and interdependence

How do two people move from casually going out together to becoming a couple in a close relationship? Smith and Mackie (2000: 431) define a close relationship as a 'connection involving strong and frequent interdependence in many areas of life'. While it is difficult – if not impossible – to identify a time or point at which this takes place, most psychologists agree that this involves moving from seeing oneself as an individual to feeling that you are a couple. One important factor in the development of close relationships is self-disclosure. This involves the sharing of increasingly personal and intimate information, which enables two people to get beyond superficial contact. Self-disclosure is important as it implies trust. It is often reciprocal – when one partner discloses it is often matched by disclosure in the other. A large amount of research has shown how self-disclosure is regulated by norms relating to what can be disclosed at which points in a relationship. These norms also show different expectations for men and women.

Developing relationships are characterized by increasing interdependence – both people in the relationship are affected by the thoughts, actions and emotions of their lover as their lives become increasingly intertwined. Smith and Mackie (2000) identify three main aspects to interdependence between two people:

1 *Affective interdependence* – this refers to the ways in which two people's feelings and emotions influence each other. If your partner is going through a tough patch, it is likely that your own feelings will be affected. You literally share in the highs and feel the lows of those you are close to.

2 *Behavioural interdependence* – means that your partner influences your actions and plans. You may spend a lot of time together and share a range of activities.

3 *Cognitive interdependence* – refers to the way in which you see the relationship. When you move from seeing yourself as an individual to part of a pair, and see yourselves as 'us' you have moved towards cognitive interdependence.

As we noted earlier, people take different pathways to intimacy: some spend a considerable amount of time getting to know each other whereas other relationships progress rapidly. In 1981, Huston, Surra, Fitzgerald and Cate studied 50 newly married couples, asking them to recollect how their relationship had developed. Huston et al. identified four distinct pathways to intimacy:

1 *Accelerated-arrested couples:* these relationships started off rapidly with both members of the couples pretty sure they would end up together, but then the relationship slowed down. They spent most of their free time together.

2 *Accelerated couples:* these followed a steady path towards commitment and marriage. They tended to share lots of household tasks.

3 *Intermediate couples:* developed their relationships slowly and without many arguments. They often led fairly separate lives and appeared less close emotionally.

4 *Prolonged couples:* these often had pretty turbulent relationships with lots of ups and downs.

From friends to lovers

As you can see, researchers have found a great deal about how people start, conduct and develop relationships in a range of different environments.

However, there are still many areas where our understanding is partial and sketchy. One of these areas is the change from friends to lovers, taken when a platonic relationship becomes romantic (Guerrero and Mongeau, 2008). Platonic to romantic relationships can also take many different paths or trajectories. Friends who have been attracted to each other may only develop or pursue a sexual relationship when they split up with other people. Alternatively, people may have loose sexual relationships ('friends with benefits') but do not see themselves as 'in a relationship'. Guerrero and Mongeau have begun to explore the processes involved in managing such relationships: they suggest that platonic, attracted friends often use 'topic avoidance' or steering clear of dangerous areas such as discussing their real relationships in order to keep the friendship platonic. One challenge for researchers within the relationship field is to explore different kinds of relationships and new definitions. This may lead to the development of models that are more inclusive.

Summary

- The matching hypothesis argues that we select partners who are similar to ourselves in the relationship 'market'. Matching is based on more factors than physical appearance
- The filter model argues that three filters operate at different times to narrow down the field of available partners into desirable potential mates.
- Reward/need theories suggest that we form relationships with people who meet our needs and who offer us rewards
- These theories put different emphasis on social and individual factors
- Close relationships develop through self-disclosure and are characterized by interdependency across different areas of life
- Pathways to intimacy are incredibly varied. An understudied area of relationships continues to be the transition from friends to lovers

Further reading

The processes involved in relationship formation are well covered in *Social Psychology* (Hogg and Vaughan, 2005) published by Pearson Education Limited.

Chapter 5

Regulating relationships

👁 Introduction

In Chapter 4, we considered some of the factors that influence whether or not two people will be attracted to each other, along with the processes involved in starting relationships. We noted that pathways to intimacy can be extremely varied: some couples get together very quickly, others take time to develop their relationship and others move from being platonic friends to lovers. In this chapter we are going to consider research and theoretical explanations that look at how couples regulate, manage and maintain their relationships. As you will know from your own experiences of relationships, they do not stay static but change, develop and deteriorate as the partners involved and the circumstances of their lives change. The idea that we can divide relationships into neat stages of formation, maintenance and breakdown is rather misleading and demonstrates the need of researchers to make relationships manageable. In practice, relationships change, shift and develop: they may experience periods of relative stability interspersed with periods of change, but they rarely stand still.

We will start this chapter by examining an important group of explanations known as **economic theories** of relationships. These theories share the view that people keep an eye on what they are putting in and getting out of a relationship in a similar way to keeping an eye on what they put in and get out of the bank. According to economic approaches, people may choose to move on if a better relationship 'deal' is offered somewhere else. Economic theories help to explain how couples keep relationships going and the decisions to stay or go when a relationship gets into difficulty. They are therefore theories of relationship regulation, considering why couples stay together or why they may decide to call it a day.

An important aspect of regulating relationships is communication. How couples communicate and deal with inevitable conflict is currently generating considerable research. We will examine research into maintenance processes including communication and dealing with conflict before moving on to consider in Chapter 6 how and why many relationships break down.

This chapter will cover:

- Economic explanations of relationship regulation including social exchange theory, interdependence theory and equity theory
- Research studies relating to these theories
- Research studies examining relationship processes including communication patterns and conflict
- Research studies examining satisfaction in relationships
- Research considering the regulation of same-sex relationships

⊙ Economic theories of relationship maintenance

Guerrero and Chavez (2005: 341) define relationship **maintenance** as 'a dynamic process that involves adapting to the changing needs and goals that characterize a relationship'. Common goals of relationship maintenance may involve keeping the relationship going, ensuring it remains in a stable condition and is satisfying for the partners, and repairing it when things go wrong (Dindia and Canary, 1993 cited in Guerrero and Chavez, 2005). In order to maintain a relationship, both partners will need to change and adapt in terms of what they expect of each other at different times.

The basis of the different economic approaches is **social exchange theory** (SET) first put forward by Homans in 1961. Economic theories fit within the experimental social perspective as they focus on the ways in which people think about their relationships and how they evaluate them. One important aspect of staying together is commitment. The study of commitment has been extensive in recent years with several different models being proposed (Kurdek, 2006). These models share the view that commitment is made up of two factors: things which keep a couple attracted to the relationship through the unique rewards offered and factors which deter them from leaving – the barriers to dissolving the relationship. The most recent of the economic theories, Rusbult's **interdependence theory** considers how commitment to relationships may relate to investments.

◉ Social exchange theory (Homans, 1961)

Homans developed SET using concepts from economics and from behavioural theories including Skinner's ideas of operant conditioning. He argued that relationships are based on give and take. He suggested that they involve **rewards**: these are pleasurable resources such as fun, company and sex which people get out of relationships. He also noted that relationships involve *costs*: these are factors in the relationship that are experienced negatively, for example arguments or loss of freedom. Homans believed that rewards and costs were subjectively defined by individuals. What may be a reward or treat for one person (such as spending time with your partner's friends or family) could be a big cost for someone else.

Homans took SET further than reward theories by noting that relationships are interactive and involve the exchange of rewards between two people. Homans argued that each relationship has an **outcome** at any time. This could be calculated by taking the rewards in the relationship and subtracting the costs. A positive outcome (or profit) was found when rewards of the relationships outweighed the costs. A negative outcome or loss would be found if the costs in the relationships outweighed the rewards. Homans argued that we run our relationships by keeping an eye on the exchange of rewards and costs.

Homans developed SET using ideas proposed by two social psychologists, Thibaut and Kelley. In *The Social Psychology of Groups* (1959), Thibaut and Kelley had argued that relationships were similar to business transactions in which people keep an eye on the 'balance sheet', seeing what is being put in and taken out. Thibaut and Kelley identified two important comparisons, which were taken up by Homans and incorporated into SET:

- **Comparison level** (CL) – this involves comparing a current relationship with a general expectation of how rewarding relationships are developed from past experiences. If the current relationship seems more rewarding than those you have previously experienced you are likely to be satisfied.

- **Comparison level for alternatives** (CL Alt) – this involves comparing the current relationship with other possible relationships on offer. If the current relationship compares favourably or there are no alternatives, you are more likely to be satisfied.

Thibaut and Kelly argued that CL Alt could be defined as 'the lowest level of outcomes in a relationship that a person will accept in the light of available opportunities' (Miell and Croghan, 1996: 283). In simple terms, this suggests that when no attractive alternatives are available, we may put up with a less than rewarding relationship.

As you can see from the above description, SET views people as basically selfish, aiming to minimize their costs in the relationship and to maximize the rewards they receive, often called the **minimax principle**. SET predicts that an individual may decide to leave a relationship if the ratio of costs and rewards cease to be positive and the relationship runs in a state of loss. This could happen if the costs in the relationship outweigh the rewards, if the CL suggests that the relationship is less rewarding than expectations or if the CL Alt offers a viable and attractive alternative.

Evidence and commentary

Sedikides, Oliver and Campbell (1994) carried out a series of studies to identify the benefits and costs involved in romantic relationships. In the first study, a group of participants were asked to provide open-ended reports/lists of the rewards and costs involved in relationships. These reports were then ranked and rated by others to provide an average score for the importance of each benefit or cost. Sedikides et al. found that the most highly ranked rewards were companionship, happiness and feeling loved. The most serious costs included stress/worrying about the relationship, and sacrifices made for the relationship (for example loss of time with other friends). They also explored the possibility of gender differences in perception of rewards and costs and found that women regarded self-understanding and self-esteem as important rewards, whereas men rated sexual gratification as more important. In terms of costs, women saw loss of identity as important whereas men were more likely to be concerned about monetary costs. However, studies have shown that both rewards and costs tend to increase as a relationship develops and two people become interdependent. (Argyle, 1996). Relationship closeness therefore goes with rewards *plus* costs rather than rewards *minus* costs.

As Sprecher (1998) notes, many of the concepts used in SET such as rewards and costs are common to other economic approaches such as **equity theory** and investment theory. SET views people as self-centred and likely to leave unrewarding relationships where costs outweigh rewards. However, it is fairly obvious that many people continue to stay in relationships that are extremely unrewarding, for example those suffering domestic abuse or violence. One reason given for this is often the amount that has been put into the relationship in the past – **investments**. SET has provided an important framework for subsequent researchers such as Caryl Rusbult to build ideas about relationships.

The fundamental assumption of SET is that we spend a good deal of time and effort monitoring our relationships. This assumption has also been challenged by Argyle (1987) who argues that people only really begin to count the costs and monitor relationships after they have become dissatisfied with them. Another fundamental assumption of SET is that people keep an eye on attractive alternatives when they are in a relationship. Steve Duck (1994: 164) disagrees with this claim saying that 'the world is always populated with an alternative partners in an objective sense. We don't see them as such, nor do we treat them as available, until we become dissatisfied with what we have'. Duck argues that people only start to consider alternatives when they become dissatisfied with their current relationship.

◉ Equity theory (Walster, Walster and Berscheid, 1978)

A second economic explanation of relationship regulation is equity theory put forward by Elaine Walster and colleagues (Walster, Walster and Berscheid, 1978). Walster et al. agree that people weigh up rewards and costs within relationships but argue that people compare their own relationship outcomes with their partner's and expect that relationships should be fair and just. Equity in a relationship is defined as 'a situation where all partners' outcomes (rewards minus costs) are proportional to their inputs or contributions to the relationship' (Hogg and Vaughan, 2005: 154). What this means in simple terms, is that what people get out of the relationship should equate to pretty much what they put in. If the relationship is unequal with one partner benefiting from the relationship but putting very little in, the relationship will be experienced as 'inequitable', which will lead to problems. This feeling of inequity will lead the 'loser' in the relationship to feel dissatisfied and the 'winner' to feel guilty. If the relationship is of relatively short duration they may simply end it. If, however, the couple have been together for a long time and both have invested in the relationship in terms of time and money, they may well be motivated to repair the relationship by restoring equity. This could be done by:

- Altering what is put into the relationship, for example putting in less (or more) effort to the relationship, or attempting to encourage the partner to put in more
- Changing the view of the rewards available in the relationship.

De Maris (2007) points to an important distinction between objective and subjective inequity. Objective inequity refers to unfairness in relation to measureable contributions such as time spent on childcare or housework, whereas subjective inequity refers to feelings of over- or under-benefiting, which are related to less tangible areas.

Evidence and commentary

Many studies have indicated that there is an association between feelings of equity and satisfaction in relationships. Walster et al. (1978) tested equity theory using a sample of 500 male and female university students who were dating. At the start of the study, each student was asked to comment on how much they and their partner were putting into the relationship and how much both were getting out of it. This enabled the researchers to give each relationship an 'equity score' from 1 to 5. Walster and colleagues returned to the students 14 weeks later and asked them if they were still going out. They were also asked about how confident they felt that they would be with their partner in one year's and five years' time. Walster and colleagues found that those who had judged their relationships as being most equitable at the start of the study were more likely to be still together than those who had judged their relationship as being less equitable. They were also much more confident that their relationship would continue.

Van Yperen and Buunk (1990) have attempted to tease out the association between equity and relationship satisfaction to determine which causes which. While it is perfectly possible that inequity in a relationship leads to dissatisfaction, it could also be that dissatisfaction or unhappiness in a relationship leads the person to put in less, producing inequity. For this reason, Van Yperen and Buunk carried out a longitudinal study that measured both equity and satisfaction at two points exactly one year apart, which were called Time 1 and Time 2.

Van Yperen and Buunk selected a sample of 736 people, made up of 259 married couples (86% of the sample) and the remainder cohabiting. The average age of participants in the study was 39 years and 70% of the couples had children. All participants responded to an advert in the local paper. Equity in the relationship was measured at Time 1/2 using an anonymous questionnaire which participants were asked to complete and return without discussion with their partner. The questionnaire used the Hatfield Global Measure (see the Thinking scientifically box below), which provided an equity score between +3 and –3. They were also asked to indicate their satisfaction with the relationship using an eight-item Likert scale developed by Buunk (1990). This included four positive statements (such as 'I feel happy when I am with my partner') and four negative statements (such as 'we have quarrels 'and 'my partner irritates me'.)

The researchers found that equity at Time 1 predicted satisfaction with the relationship especially for women at Time 2. The correlation between equity and satisfaction was .44 in women taking part in the study. Equity was less strongly related to satisfaction in men with a correlation of .20. This implies that equity is more strongly related to happiness in women. This suggestion has been confirmed by other research. De Maris (2007) assessed the importance of equity in relation to marital dissatisfaction and later breakdown. Using a sample of 1500 North American couples, he found that a woman's sense of being under-benefited was most important in predicting later breakdown. Together these findings imply that equity is indeed important in relationships but probably more so for women than men (Van Yperen and Buunk, 1990). Miell and Croghan (1996) argue that the equity principle is more important in western, individualistic cultures and less important in collectivist cultures.

Thinking scientifically → How can we measure equity?

Equity is a slippery concept and there are very wide differences in what couples see as fair in relationships. For this reason, researchers do not attempt to assess objective equity but are interested in subjective views or feelings of equity.

Researchers have devised a range of measures to assess equity within personal relationships. One commonly used approach is the Global Measure of Equity such as that devised by Hatfield, Traupmann-Pillemer and O'Brien (1990). This asks participants to indicate what kind of deal they are getting in the relationship in the light of what they and their partners are putting in and getting out. This is measured using a single *equity score* from +3 (I am getting a much better deal than my partner) through zero (We are both getting an equally good deal) to –3 (My partner is getting a much better deal than me). This approach gives a quick and simple snapshot of the overall feelings in the relationship at that specific time. Of course responses may be influenced by the mood of the couple at the time as well as by recent events.

Other measures of equity are more detailed and extensive, providing a 'fine-grained' assessment. The Traupmann-Utne-Hatfield scale (Traupmann, Petersen, Utne and Hatfield,1981) asks participants to assess their own inputs and outcomes and their partner's inputs and outcomes in relation to four different areas of their relationship: personal concerns, emotional concerns, day to day practical concerns and opportunities gained and lost. In total, 22 questions are used to measure own inputs and 24 questions relate to partners' inputs. This clearly takes much more time to complete but is a far wider measurement of equity across different areas of the relationship.

This measurement dilemma is not just restricted to measuring equity. You may recall that a similar discussion took place in Chapter 3 regarding the measurement of attachment style via a single-item versus multi-item psychometric test.

⊙ Interdependence theory (Rusbult and Van Lange, 1996)

Our final economic explanation of relationship regulation is interdependence theory. This theory has grown out of Caryl Rusbult's investment model (1983). According to Rusbult, investments and **commitment** are the keys to understanding how and why couples stay together. Investments are things that have been put into the relationship that cannot be got back out. Rusbult distinguishes between two types of investment:

- *Intrinsic investments* – are those that are put directly into the relationship, for example time, or disclosure of personal information about the self

- *Extrinsic investments* – these are shared things that may be lost such as your prized vinyl collection, holiday photos and a network of mutual friends.

According to interdependence theory, couples who are committed to a relationship stay together because they become increasingly more reliant on each other to meet their needs. This increasing interdependence is experienced subjectively as the feeling of commitment. Commitment comes from three factors.

1 The first of these is satisfaction with the relationship, which primarily comes from rewards gained from the partner
2 The second aspect of commitment is the investments that have been put into the relationship
3 The third factor is the quality of available alternatives. When these are perceived as low, commitment to the relationship is likely to be higher.

Together, feelings of satisfaction and investments contribute to commitment, which acts as the glue that holds relationships together. The difference between this approach and exchange theory/equity theory is the emphasis on past investments rather than a focus on current rewards or fairness. As the research studies below indicate, investments appear to be very important in helping to understand why people stay in relationships that are unrewarding and may even be abusive offering little but costs!

Evidence and commentary

Interdependence theory has generated considerable research and interest. Many studies have supported the claims of the model and shown that investments are very important in understanding why couples stay together. Impett, Beals and Peplau (2003) tested the investment model using a prospective study of a large sample of married couples over an 18-month period. They found that commitment to the marriage by both partners predicted relationship stability, supporting Rusbult's model. In a substantial meta-analysis of 52 studies using a total of 11,582 people, Le and Agnew (2003) found support for both claims of Rusbult's model. The three variables – satisfaction, alternatives and investments – were strongly related to commitment and commitment was indeed the best predictor of relationship stability.

Researchers have also applied investment theory to explain why people may choose to stay in relationships that appear to be wholly unrewarding, for example those involving neglect, abuse or domestic violence. Rhatigan and Axsom (2006) studied a group of women living in a refuge and found that each of Rusbult's three factors contributed to women's commitment to stay with their partner, supporting the investment model. Jerstad (2005) extended this work by considering commitment in both men and women who were in violent dating relationships. She found that investments, notably the amount of time and effort put into the relationship, were the most important predictor of whether or not someone would stay with a violent partner. Those who had experienced the most violence were often the most committed – almost as if their previous experiences were 'investments' which would be rendered worthless if they left.

Summary

- Relationship maintenance involves keeping relationships stable and satisfying and repairing them when things go wrong
- Economic theories view relationships as a series of exchanges
- SET argues that we weigh up rewards and costs to establish if a relationship is in profit or loss
- We also compare our relationships with those in the past (CL) and other alternatives (CL Alt)
- SET focuses on current rewards and ignores the role of previous investments
- Equity theory argues that couples want their relationships to be fair, with rewards proportional to inputs
- Longitudinal studies of dating, cohabiting and married couples have shown that inequity is associated with unhappiness and later relationship breakdown especially for women
- Rusbult's investment theory argues that commitment predicts relationship stability
- Commitment comes from satisfaction, investments and the quality of alternatives
- Studies have shown that investments are important in exploring why people stay in unrewarding relationships

◉ Maintenance processes

As the above illustrates, economic theories focus on how people think about their relationships and decide if they are worth the effort. However, they tell us relatively little about other aspects of maintaining relationships such as feelings. They also ignore the day to day processes that take place in relationships and how people run the day to day activities. Recent research into communication and conflict is showing us how important these factors appear to be in regulating relationships and maintaining satisfaction. Studies of communication are also proving to be extremely important in understanding and predicting how and when some couples may split up.

Communication and conflict

Conflict is pretty inevitable in relationships and comes from a range of different sources. These may include internal factors that come from the two people involved (for example one partner becomes ill and unable to put as much effort into the relationship). Conflict may also arise from external factors such as changes to work responsibilities, financial pressures or redundancy. Finally, social norms regarding the division of household labour may also be sources of conflict for many couples. What do we know about conflict and relationships? As we will explore, research indicates that it is not the presence of conflict but how the partners deal with it that appears to be most important in understanding relationship survival. Tran and Simpson (2009) argue that 'the fate of any relationship – whether happy or haunted – depends on how partners think, feel and behave in difficult situations'.

Rusbult and Zembrodt (1983) classified some of the ways that couples deal with conflict. They identified four different kinds of behavioural strategies that partners may use to deal with disclosures of dissatisfaction from their partner. They divided these into active strategies (those which involved taking action of some sort) and passive strategies (those which involve inaction). Further to this, they subdivided the strategies into those which are constructive (helpful) and those which are destructive (unhelpful) to the relationship. This provides four different ways of dealing with conflict which are summarized in Table 5.1.

	Active	Passive
Constructive	*Voice* involves discussing and working at the problem. This is an active, constructive strategy which aims to tackle the dissatisfaction	*Loyalty* involves waiting for the relationship to improve. It demonstrates a desire to stay with the relationship
Destructive	*Exit* involves getting out of the relationship. This strategy may be constructive for the person who takes it but is ultimately destructive for the relationship	*Neglect* involves ignoring or refusing to discuss the problem. This indicates or is often interpreted as a lack of concern or commitment to the partner and the relationship

Table 5.1 Dealing with conflict (Rusbult and Zembrodt, 1983)

Sex differences in dealing with conflict

Rusbult and Zembrodt's classification is helpful in getting us to think about the different ways people have of dealing with relationships issues and problems. Of course, the two people involved in the relationship may not share the same approach to dealing with conflict. If one person's preferred approach is to discuss the problem, whereas their partner's favoured approach is to ignore it, this may lead to additional problems. Research by Rusbult (Rusbult et al., 1991) has indicated that there are broad sex differences in use of these strategies: for example, women are more likely to respond to relationship problems by wanting to talk about them (Voice) whereas men are more likely to respond by withdrawal or distance. These approaches are probably learned and reinforced through gender socialization which still encourages girls to express feelings more than boys. These differences can, however, lead women to label men as not caring or rejecting and men to view women's approach as nagging/threatening. As Smith and Mackie note, these differences provide a 'rich soil for the seeds of misunderstanding' (2000: 456). There are important implications here for relationship counselling: helping to interpret and use different communication patterns may well help couples to work through conflicts more positively.

Attachment style and conflict

Perhaps more important than gender differences are differences based on attachment style. As we indicated in Chapter 3, attachment style is an important factor in understanding how people conduct their relationships and deal with conflict. Simpson, Rholes and Phillips (1996) have argued that conflict situations are ideal ways of seeing attachment styles in action. This is because attachment behaviours aren't always obvious but are likely to come to the fore when people are under stress or in challenging situations. A range of studies indicate differences between those with secure and insecure attachment styles. Securely attached people are more likely to act constructively when conflicts arise (Kobak and Hazan, 1991) and are more likely to accommodate their partner and change their behaviour (Simpson et al., 1996). Those who are insecure tend to deal with conflict in less constructive ways such as outbursts of negative emotion (Levy and Davis, 1988). A wealth of research is now emerging which explores differences in attachment style.

Simpson et al. (1996) examined a sample of dating couples who were asked to discuss a minor or major relationship problem while being recorded by concealed cameras. Before this, each participant completed a measurement of attachment style. The researchers found – in line with their predictions – that those who were classed as ambivalent experienced more stress and anxiety during the conversation. This was especially noted in women who scored highly on anxiety. The researchers argued that people with ambivalent attachment styles are hyper-vigilant (aware) of their partner's emotional availability and will tend to become anxious easily, which may spill over into negative behaviours such as anger and clinginess during arguments and negotiations. In contrast, those who had been classed as avoidant tended to behave with less warmth and supportiveness. This pattern was most marked in men. The researchers argue that this pattern comes from the childhood strategy of shutting off their own emotions in the face of parents who do not respond to them.

In an interesting recent study, Simpson and Tran (2009) have attempted to bring together the predictions of attachment theory and interdependence theory to see how these two factors working together may help us to understand relationship conflict.

Thinking scientifically → **Research study: Tran and Simpson (2009)**

Tran and Simpson examined how attachment style and commitment work together in relationship conflict. A sample of 74 married couples took part in two videotaped discussions in which both members of the couple challenged their partner about an aspect of their behaviour that they were unhappy with. Previous to this, all participants completed Brennan, Clark and Shaver's (1998) Experiences of Close Relationships Scale, Rusbult's (1983) Investment Commitment Scale and Hendrick's (1988) Relationship Satisfaction Scale. The videotaped discussion was coded by observers and analyses examined how the two measurements – attachment and commitment – worked together.

Tran and Simpson found that insecurely attached couples experienced greater distress during the discussions and felt more rejected after the discussion. Those with avoidant styles were more destructive than those with ambivalent styles. However, commitment to the relationship mediated these effects. Insecurely attached individuals who were highly committed to the relationship experienced fewer feelings of rejection and were more accepting of their partners after the discussion, leading Tran and Simpson to conclude that 'commitment and attachment jointly affect how people feel'.

John Gottman, working in the United States, has spent a considerable amount of time looking at factors that may predict which couples will stay together and which split up. Gottman has noted that while unhappiness is important in splitting up, it does not always predict which couples will divorce. In order to study communication in couples, Gottman has devised a unique combination of methods in which couples carry out video-recorded conversations about a range of topics in the laboratory while monitored for physiological responses. Longitudinal studies of couples over many years have begun to 'fill in the gaps' and help us to understand which aspects of communication may be associated with happy and unhappy relationships.

Gottman's longitudinal American study of 197 couples began in 1983. Each member of the couple was assessed to measure their satisfaction with the relationship using two scales designed to measure marital satisfaction (Time 1). Of this sample, a total of 85 couples were selected for further study: this second sample consisted of a range of couples across the whole happiness/satisfaction spectrum. This group were studied again four years later in 1987 (Time 2) and then again every year for the next ten years. In the 1992 follow-up, Gottman and Levenson identified a pattern of negative communication which was shown by unhappy couples. This pattern was made up of four different components, which the researchers termed 'The four Horseman of the Apocalypse' as they appeared to signify relationship doom. These factors were:

1   Criticism – verbally attacking or belittling the partner

2 Defensiveness – claiming their own behaviour was acceptable or justified

3 Contempt – showing scorn for their partner

4 Stonewalling – refusing to acknowledge or discuss problems in the relationship.

Criticism met by defensiveness or stonewalling is also characteristic of those with anxious-avoidant attachment pairings. This pattern seems to be emerging from different studies as extremely significant in communication, unhappiness and later relationship breakdown. In Gottman's later follow-up of the same sample of couples in 2002, a total of 21 had gone on to divorce. Gottman and Levenson have investigated how these communication factors relate to time of divorce. We will consider Gottman's **two factor model** of relationship dissolution in Chapter 6.

Unhappy couples may also fall into cycles of conflict. This happens when one partner responds to the other's negative or destructive behaviour with a destructive reaction that then leads to a deterioration, arguments and slanging matches. However, evidence suggests that constructive ways of handling conflict can be taught to couples and these appear to have dramatic effects on relationship happiness and survival. In one German study, Hahlweg et al. (1998) trained 55 couples in effective communication and problem-solving using a six session programme while a control group of 17 matched couples received no training. Three years later in a follow-up, the experimental group were significantly less likely to have divorced and reported higher levels of relationships satisfaction, indicating the importance of such programmes.

◉ Relationship satisfaction

Rusbult et al. (1991) argue that there are different kinds of maintenance behaviours which couples use to keep relationships going smoothly. Constructive behaviours may include:

- *Accommodative behaviour:* this involves responding in a constructive way when your partner behaves inconsiderately or rudely, rather than escalating into arguments or conflict
- *Willingness to sacrifice:* this involves subduing your own goals or aims, or compromising in the interests of relationship harmony

- *Derogation of alternatives:* a third strategy used to keep relationships healthy is downplaying attractive alternatives or turning a blind eye to other offers.

Which factors appear to be important in terms of commitment and satisfaction and which characteristics mark out relationships that stand the test of time? Smith and Mackie (2000: 463) identify two factors that appear to be important. These are firstly, that the relationship meets many of the needs of the two people involved and secondly, that it provides both partners with 'a sense of relatedness and connectedness', a special place in which they are valued as a unique and irreplaceable individual.

The social level of relationships

Relationships do not exist within a vacuum. Most couples have surrounding networks of friends and family and these seem to be important in under-standing satisfaction and happiness. Family members and friends may help when couples get into difficulties by offering practical help (such as childcare) and emotional support for partners. Karney and Bradbury (1995) examined nearly 200 variables to establish which seemed to be linked to relationship satisfaction and stability. They found that relation-ship stability was linked to education and to employment: better educated partners who had jobs were more likely to have stable relationships. They also found a strong relationship between satisfaction and support networks: both members of a couple were happier and experienced greater satisfaction when they had mutual friends. This has led Karney and Bradbury to conclude that 'marriage is more than a union of two individuals: it includes … an overlap between two larger networks of people' (page 527). Relationships are more than simply alliances between two people.

⊙ Regulating same-sex relationships

As we noted in Chapter 1, same-sex relationships are likely to exist within a different social context to heterosexual relationships. In many cases, they are developed without family support and may even be formed without the knowledge of family members of either of the couple. Kurdek's study (2004) found that compared to heterosexual couples, the gay couples in his sample received much less support from their families than heterosexual couples. However, they received greater social support from their friends and social networks than did heterosexual couples.

Research studies have pointed to the importance of both equality and equity in regulating same-sex relationships. As we noted in Chapter 1, same-sex couples are likely to divide household work in very different ways to heterosexual couples, lesbian couples tending to share tasks and gay men splitting tasks by negotiation. Kurdek (1995) carried out a longitudinal study of relationship quality in a sample of 61 gay and 42 lesbian couples of differing ages. Kurdek found that lesbian partners rated equality as more important than gay men and commitment and satisfaction in lesbian relationships were strongly related to levels of equality. Similarly, Dwyer (2000) argues that lesbians put a considerable value on equity within a relationship. Equity and equality may well be important to lesbian couples as they reject the traditional ideas of hetero-sexual relationships which are often characterized by power differences between men and women.

As we noted in Chapter 1, an important feature of same-sex relation-ships is the lack of gender differences. These are quite apparent when we examine how same-sex couples deal with conflict. While the same issues – money, affection, sex, housework and driving behaviour – cause conflict in both gay and straight relationships, studies have indicated that gay couples appear to be better at dealing with conflict than heterosexual partners who often have very different communication styles. Kurdek (2004) carried out a longitudinal study in which he compared samples of 53 lesbian and 80 gay cohabiting couples, with 80 cohabiting heterosexual couples with children. He measured conflict resolution, examining the use of two strategies to solve conflicts:

- *Demand/withdrawal* – takes place when one partner makes demands for action or change and the other responds by withdrawing further into the relationship
- *Positive communication* – supporting of the partner, warmth.

Kurdek found that gay male couples used fewer 'demand / withdrawal' communication patterns and more positive communication than the heterosexual couples in the sample. The lesbian couples also used more positive communication patterns than the heterosexual couples. These findings have led Kurdek to conclude that gay couples are better at resolving conflict than heterosexual partners as they do not descend into a typically gendered pattern of female demands and male withdrawal.

Studies of very long-term relationships have indicated that similar qualities and factors are important in satisfaction for both same-sex and heterosexual couples. Mackey, Diemer and O' Brien (2004) studied relationship satisfaction in a sample of 108 couples – both gay and straight – who had been together for thirty years or more. They were studied using in-depth interviews, and regression analysis was used to identify the important factors associated with relationship satisfaction. Mackey et al. found that two factors emerged as predicting satisfaction in the couples overall. These were:

- Intimate communication between the couples: happy couples were those who continue to share intimate information and to talk with their partners.
- The containment of relationship conflict: couples who dealt with arguments but did not allow these to dominate the relationship were happiest.

These factors were important for all the couples in the sample, suggesting that happiness and success in very long-term relationships comes down to the same issues whether the couple are gay or straight.

Thinking scientifically →
Studying same-sex relationships

Kurdek (2005) has identified a range of challenges for researchers studying same-sex relationships. These challenges arise due to the hidden, unseen nature of gay relationships. Because couples may face abuse or discrimination, they are less likely to come forward to participate in research. One challenge is therefore obtaining a representative sample of same-sex couples. Most studies considered here have used convenience samples, which are generally composed of well-educated, white same-sex couples, often those opting for civil marriages, and it is unclear how representative these findings may be of the wider gay and lesbian population. Secondly, many studies rely on self-report measures of relationships, which are likely to yield socially desirable answers. Kurdek argues that future research should focus on using less-biased measurements such as behavioural observations in order to increase validity.

◉ Chapter summary

- Conflict is inevitable in longer-term relationships
- How couples deal with conflict is important for relationship survival
- Behavioural strategies include Voice, Loyalty, Neglect and Exit
- Strategies may differ between men and women and may also relate to attachment style
- Gottman has identified four communication factors that signify relationship doom
- Demand/withdrawal patterns or criticism/stonewalling seem to be the most negative patterns
- Longitudinal studies show that couples can be trained to deal with and resolve conflict constructively. Training programmes lead to significantly less divorce
- Satisfying long-term relationships include couples who communicate intimately and who have good ways of containing and dealing with conflict
- Outside factors including social networks of families and friends are also related to satisfaction in relationships
- Gay couples receive less support for their relationships from families but more support from friends
- Equity and equality are important factors in same-sex relationships
- Gay couples are better at managing and resolving conflict than heterosexual couples

◉ Further reading

Excellent coverage of communication and conflict is given in Smith, E. and Mackie, D. (2000) *Social Psychology*, published by Psychology Press.

Chapter 6

Breakdown of relationships

👁 Introduction

An old joke goes something like: 'What is the best predictor of divorce?' The answer, of course, is marriage. Every year thousands of relationships end. Some of these endings may be relatively stress free, with both members of the couple agreeing amicably to go their separate ways. But others may create emotional havoc in the lives of those involved. While there may be fewer practical barriers, such as shared property or children, to ending a short-term relationship, these splits can still be emotionally devastating.

In this chapter, we shall examine psychological research considering relationship breakdown. There are two main focuses of research in this area: why relationships break down and how breakdown takes place. These two questions have been attractive to social psychologists, as they are relatively easy to study using the quantitative and statistical tools which predominate within modern, social psychological research. The perspectives we have covered in earlier chapters make their own predictions and offer some insights into why couples split up. Economic theories focus on issues of rewards, investments and fairness. Evolutionary theories locate the cause of break-ups in the different predispositions brought to relationships by men and women, whereas attachment theorists look for reasons related to early relationships and internal working models. As you read through this chapter, you may wish to think about how the theories and studies discussed fit within these broader perspectives on relationships.

Relationship breakdown is an experience that can differ very widely between individuals. Human experience is difficult to capture using quantitative methods and some social psychologists have used qualitative methods to consider how people experience, understand and justify relationship splits. Although some relationship splits may involve agreement of both parties, quite a lot are instigated by one partner who wants out of the relationship. This brings us to a fundamental issue in relationship breakdown: here, more than anywhere else in the study of relationships, experiences are unique and generalizations may fail to capture this.

This chapter will cover:
- The ending of short-term relationships
- The prevalence of relationship breakdown and divorce in western cultures
- Barriers to dissolving long-term relationships
- The impact of individual factors including attachment type and parental divorce
- Breaking the rules: infidelity and relationship breakdown
- The role of communication and conflict in relationship breakdown
- Gottman's two factor model of relationship breakdown
- Breakdown of same-sex relationships
- Phase models of how relationships end

Understanding relationship breakdown: a conceptual framework

As we noted in Chapter 1, early research was criticized heavily for focusing on the two individuals involved but ignoring the social context surrounding relationships. In order to begin to understand relationship breakdown, we should consider factors operating a number of different levels:

- *The social level* – focuses on the context, environment and wider culture. Most relationships exist within a network of families and friends who may offer support when the relationship is in difficulties or take sides with one partner in the event of a split. However, as we noted in Chapter 1, many same-sex couples receive much less by way of family support and help. As well as a social network, all relationships exist within a wider culture. Western societies have seen an increase in the acceptability and ease of divorce over the past forty years. In order to understand relationship breakdown, we must consider how social norms and values influence a couple to stay together or enable them to separate.

- *The individual level* – focuses on the characteristics and personalities of the two people involved in the relationship. Duck (1992) refers to these characteristics as 'pre-disposing personal factors' that may make a relationship inherently unstable. One important **predisposing factor** relates to early childhood experience and attachment style.

- *The dyadic level* – focuses on the interactions between the two partners and the ways in which they communicate. Events such as leaving home, starting university and changes to the family such as the birth of children generate stress and may a put relationship under serious strain. These are often referred to as 'precipitating factors' (Duck, 1992). How a couple deals with stressful events, how they negotiate, communicate and deal with conflict is also important. Negative communication patterns, such as Gottman and Levenson's Four Horsemen of the Apocalypse (1992) may lead relationships into difficulties or prevent conflict being resolved. These factors operate at the dyadic level as they consider how the two main actors in the relationship operate as a couple.

◉ The end of the affair: Why do short-term relationships end?

Every day, large numbers of casual or short-term relationships end. As we noted in Chapter 3, many of these fizzle out without every really getting off the ground. Research studies have pointed to the importance of dissimilarity in understanding why dating couples split up. Hill, Rubin and Peplau (1976) carried out a two-year study of 231 heterosexual student couples living around Boston, Massachusetts. Across this period of time 45% of the couples split up. The vast majority of the break-ups in this sample (85%) were one-sided, instigated by one person who wanted the split while the partner was unwilling. The researchers compared those who had stayed together and those who had split up in relation to demo-graphic similarity. They found that couples who separated were more likely to be dissimilar in educational level, intelligence and physical attrac-tiveness whereas those who stayed together appeared to be matched on these attributes. Similarity of religion and attitudes to having children were less important. This study is broadly in agreement with the predictions made in Chapter 4 by Kerckhoff and Davis's filter model.

Baxter (1986) asked 157 students who had just split up with a partner to write a story about the reasons for the split. He found a number of reasons that reoccurred in many of the narratives. These included:

- A lack of freedom or autonomy – feeling tied down and wanting greater independence
- A lack of similarity between the two partners – discovering little in common
- The partner was not open about feelings and emotions
- The partner did not offer emotional support
- The relationship was unfair or inequitable
- Partners were not spending enough time together
- The 'magic' or romance had gone out of the relationship.

These reasons demonstrate the distinction between individual and dyadic factors introduced earlier. Some reasons, such as feeling tied down, relate to the individual whereas others – such as lack of similarity or the relationship being unfair – relate to how well the partners meet each other's needs or fit together as their expectations change and develop. Baxter's factors are also consistent with Kerchkhoff and Davis's filter theory. Couples who find themselves poorly matched or having different needs may decide to end the relationship.

Reason for splitting up	Female	Male
Desire for greater independence	44%	27%
Dissimilarity/not enough in common	32%	27%
Lack of support/partner undermines self-esteem	33%	19%
Lack of intimacy	31%	8%
Absence of passion/the magic has gone	3%	19%

Table 6.1 Reasons for ending a short-term relationship (Baxter 1986)

Baxter also analysed his data to compare the reasons given by men and women (see Table 6.1). In some areas these were very similar: both sexes agreed that dissimilarity and having little in common was an important cause of break-up as was the desire for greater freedom. However, there were also gender differences in the reasons for splitting up. Women were more likely to end a relationship due to of a lack of intimacy or support, suggesting their emotional expectations were not met. In contrast, men were more concerned with the loss of excitement and 'magic' in a relationship. These gender differences are consistent with the predictions of the evolutionary perspective: women appear to be concerned with the emotional quality of the relationship whereas men appear to be focused on the loss of excitement and passion. Baxter's data also offers some support for equity theory, as a lack of fairness/equity was one of the factors that led to dissatisfaction here.

👁 Breaking up in long-term relationships

Social context

In marriages, the formal ending of a relationship takes place through legal separation or divorce. In many western countries such as the United States and Great Britain, divorce has become much more common over the past forty years. As you can see from Figure 6.1, the number of divorces in the UK was low in the 1970s but rose rapidly across the decade and throughout the 1980s, reaching a peak in 1993. Since then, the number of people divorcing has declined, reflecting the smaller number of people who choose to get married. The current divorce figures have levelled out at between 150,000 and 160,000 per year, which stands at roughly one in three marriages. The likelihood of a marriage ending in divorce is even higher when this is a second or third marriage for one or both partners (ONS, 2009).

The increase in divorce rate has been associated with a variety of social changes that have led to divorce becoming practically easier, more socially acceptable and financially possible. The relaxing of divorce laws, which began with the 1969 Divorce Act, made divorce easier for unhappy couples. This Act allowed divorces to take place without the agreement of both partners if a relationship was believed by one of the couple to have irretrievably broken down. This could be demonstrated through evidence of adultery, separation of the couple, desertion or unreasonable behaviour by one partner. In addition, the increasing participation of women in education and the job market has led to greater financial independence, making women less likely to stay in unsatisfactory relationships.

As we noted in Chapter 1, there has been a marked increase in the past 25 years in the number of people living together in western societies

Persons divorcing per thousand married population

Divorce rate, England and Wales

Figure 6.1 Divorces, rate per thousand, 1971 to 2006
(*Source:* ONS, 2009. Reproduced under the terms of the Click-Use License)

(Brehmn, 1992). While precise statistics do not exist in the same form as those from the Office for National Statistics (ONS), evidence suggests that cohabiters are more likely to separate than married couples. This may be because cohabiters differ from married couples in several ways: they are likely to be younger and are lower in religious commitment. As well as this they are likely to have fewer children (Hoem and Hoem, 1988). All three of these factors are associated with a greater likelihood of relationship breakdown.

Barriers to ending long-term relationships

One of the distinctions between short- and longer-term relationships relates to the degree of interdependence between the couple and the extent of the forces that keep them together. Although the experience of splitting up may be as painful, there are fewer practical barriers to separating when a couple do not live together, have children or share property. However, these factors may act as deterrents and keep them together when the relationship gets into difficulties.

Kurdek (2006) has demonstrated how these forces operate in both heterosexual and same-sex relationships. He studied a sample of 33 gay cohabiting couples, 52 lesbian cohabiting couples and 72 heterosexual married couples all in long-term (mean 14 years) relationships. Each member of the couple was asked to list up to five factors that they really valued in the relationship and five factors that deterred them from splitting up. They then rated these for importance.

Kurdek identified two main classes of deterrents to leaving a long-term relationship:

- The first set was the same factors that were listed as attractions and were things about the relationship that would be missed such as intimacy, companionship and support. Typical answers were statements such as 'He is my best friend 'or 'We help each other through tough times'.
- The second set were barriers to leaving the relationship, including moral disapproval (the feeling that you ought to stay in the relationship), impact on children, fear of loneliness and the feelings of family/friends who may be hurt or disappointed.

Kurdek found that heterosexual couples systematically rated the second set of factors such as family, children and moral values as strong deterrents against leaving the relationship. In contrast, same-sex couples were more concerned with the strength of the first set of factors: loss of intimacy was an important deterrent which kept them together. Kurdek argues that the shorter-lived nature of cohabiting relationships reflects simply the 'absence of institutionalized barriers that help to stabilize a relationship' (2006: 533).

Individual factors in relationship breakdown

Individual factors can loosely be seen as the qualities or characteristics brought by the two partners to the relationship. These are often known as predisposing personal factors (Duck, 1992). Karney and Bradbury (1997) examined nearly 200 variables to establish which of these factors were linked with relationship satisfaction and relationship breakdown. They found that lasting relationships were linked to education and to employment. Better educated partners who had jobs were more likely to have 'stable' and lasting relationships. In contrast, a number of factors predicted relationship breakdown including:

- an unhappy childhood
- neuroticism, anxiety and instability in one or both partners

- negative behaviours (for example gambling or drinking) by one partner.

Other studies have shown a link between age at marriage and later divorce. The younger two people are when they marry, the greater is the likelihood that their relationship will end in divorce (Mott and Moore, 1979). Having children at a young age is also linked with later divorce (McLanahan and Bumpass, 1988). Both these factors are more common in people whose parents divorced when they were young.

Terling-Watt (2001) examined the factors that predicted later divorce in men and women: 5888 married people took part in a baseline interview and were followed up five years later to see who had subsequently split up. Terling-Watt found that the factors that predicted divorce were very similar for women and men. These factors included:

- Early attachments: for women, parental divorce and a poor relationship with their mother were most significant. For men, a poor or problematic relationship with their father was important
- Areas of conflict such as disagreements over sex and money
- Loneliness and a lack of companionship in the relationship.

In contrast to Baxter's study, this research implies that the same factors are important to both men and women in the ending of longer-term relationships. They also point strongly to the importance of attachment style in understanding breakdown.

The findings from statistical studies are relatively robust and there is now an online 'marriage calculator' which calculates the likelihood of any relationship ending in divorce (Astana and Campbell, 2009). The calculator works by asking people to input their age, educational level and age at marriage (the key predicting variables). Those who have devised the calculator argue these key variables predict pretty accurately the likelihood of two people staying together or splitting up.

Statistical studies provide us with the facts about who is likely to split up, but they give us very little explanation as to why these factors are important – the 'story' behind the facts. For example, we know that younger people are statistically more likely to split up, but this could be for a range of different reasons. It may be that people who are more impulsive marry at a young age and it is this factor that leads to later breakdown. Alternatively it could be younger partners are more likely to change and mature as they grow older, leading them to grow apart.

Attachments and the impact of parental divorce

The developmental perspective, which we considered in Chapter 3, argues that our early attachments with caregivers and parents provide us with two frameworks or constructs that affect our later adult relationships:

1 A characteristic **attachment type**: This is mainly developed from our early childhood relationship with parents/caregivers but may also be influenced by the stress of life events and family disruption in later childhood notably parental divorce (Zimmerman et al., 2000). Attachment types come in three main forms, secure, insecure-avoidant or insecure-resistant.

2 An **internal working model** of relationships. This acts like a template for future relationships telling us what to expect and providing ideas about how relationships work, and about trust and commitment. The working models of those with secure attachments are likely to be more positive than those with insecure attachments.

As we noted in Chapter 3, the continuity hypothesis argues that those with insecure childhood attachment types will be most at risk of adult relationship breakdown, a view supported by Terling-Watt's 2001 study. However, we also noted that early attachment styles could be changed in both directions. Events such as parental death or divorce could lead to insecurity and strong relationships in adulthood could lead to 'earned security'.

What about the impact of parental divorce on later relationships? Newspaper headlines regularly report the 'link' between having divorced parents and splitting up. Statistically, studies indicate that children whose parents have divorced are more likely to experience divorce in their adult relationships (Amato, 1999). Wallenstein and Lewis (1998) suggest that parental divorce may have different impacts on different people. They may carry forward a template of failed marital relationships and wonder about their own abilities for commitment and their capacity for love. They may also be more likely to end an unsatisfactory relationship knowing that this is possible. Alternatively, parental divorce can lead adults to become more determined to work at their own adult relation-ships, to be more sensitive to relationship difficulties and committed to solving them.

In order to investigate different responses to parental divorce, Shulman, Scharf, Lumer and Maurer (2001) examined the impact of parental divorce on young adults' relationships using a sample of 51 Israeli adults aged between 19 and 29 whose parents had divorced when they were young. Participants took part in an interview in which they discussed their current relationship and their parents' divorce. The interview started with the participant being asked to talk about their current relationship in response to an open question 'What kind of person is your partner and how do you get along together?' These interviews were tape-recorded and then rated for different factors.

In the second part of the interview they were asked a series of open questions about their parents' divorce such as 'What do you remember about the divorce?' and 'What do you think about it today?' Again these responses were rated on a 5-point scale by two observers working independently. Finally, participants completed questionnaires, one relating to their own relationship and the second covering the amount of conflict between their parents during and after the split.

Shulman et al. found that parental divorce was not necessarily linked to poorer adult relationships. Those who had experienced traumatic and emotional parental conflict reported higher levels of intimacy and happiness in their current relationship. What seemed to be most important was how well the individual had come to terms with the divorce and resolved the issues. In keeping with Main, Kaplan and Cassidy's (1985) idea of 'earned security', those who had worked through the issues and could speak about the past in a secure/earned secure way were happiest. Shulman et al. argued that parental divorce does not have to have a negative impact on later adult relationships. It can make children more sensitive to problems in their own relationships and more committed to solving problems before the relationship breaks down. In this framework, parental divorce may lead to a transformation of family relationships, but this need not be negative.

Thinking scientifically → The conversion of qualitative data to quantitative format

Shulman et al.'s study demonstrates how rich qualitative data derived from interviews can be rated for specific features in order to make comparisons and to draw conclusions. In this study, the interview started with the participant being asked to talk about their current relationship in response to an open question 'What kind of person is your partner and how do you get along together?' These interviews were tape-recorded and then rated using a 5-point scale devised by

Feeney and Noller (1991). Two separate observers rated each narrative for five different criteria:

- How much the person idealized their partner
- The closeness of the friendship between the couple
- Problems in the relationship
- Trust of the partner
- Enjoyment in the relationship

In the second part of the interview, participants were asked to discuss their parent's divorce and these narratives were rated, again on the following criteria:

- How well the person was able to see the divorce from the viewpoint of both parents
- The sense of loss in the narrative both in the past and present
- Feelings of anger towards either parent
- Lack of memory

This study demonstrates how rich, qualitative data obtained from interview transcripts can be coded and converted into a quantitative format that enables comparisons to be made between narratives. In order to achieve a high level of reliability (that is, agreement) between raters, considerable discussion of the rating criteria would be needed. In both cases, the degree of agreement between the two raters was from 68% to just under 90% for each narrative.

Breaking the rules: infidelity and relationship breakdown

According to the evolutionary perspective, men and women bring different agendas and needs to their relationships. These are best seen as inbuilt predispositions to behave in certain ways that brought reproductive advantages in the past. This perspective claims that men are most likely to benefit from pursuing both short- and long-term relationships in order to produce as many offspring as possible. In contrast, women seek commitment from a single partner who will provide resources for offspring. This theory therefore predicts that these different agendas effectively put heterosexual men and women in conflict with different relationship needs. It also predicts that sexual jealousy and infidelity will be important factors in relationship breakdown.

Most western heterosexual relationships (with the exception of some religious groups) adopt a model of sexual exclusivity – they expect the relationship to involve two people only and outside sexual activity is viewed as 'cheating'. When Diana, Princess of Wales was interviewed by

Martin Bashir in 1995, she said that there were three people in her marriage. This comment was instantly understood by most people as breaking the rule of exclusivity which governs relationships. It is therefore not surprising that 'cheating' is one of the most common causes of divorce (Amato and Rogers, 1997). Infidelity (or adultery) was one of the four defining factors in the 1969 Divorce Act and was cited as a reason for divorce by 11.8 % men and 20.2% women in ONS statistics (ONS, 2005).

Affairs most often happen at transition points in the lifecycle, such as following birth of a first child or after children have left home (Pittman, 1989). The issue of infidelity is one of the most challenging for researchers to investigate. Few people wish to talk openly about such a sensitive topic at the time, leading researchers to devise ethical ways of studying this area. One method that can be used involves responses to hypothetical situations using *vignettes* (Shackelford, 1998). Shackelford studied a sample of 107 newly married couples who each took part in an interview. They were asked to respond to descriptions of six levels of infidelity from relatively trivial (for example partner flirting drunkenly with someone) to moderate (quick grope at an office party) to serious (an extended sexual affair that has gone on for a time and involved lying). Shackelford asked his participants to think about each scenario and then state the probability that it would end their marriage. For example, a probability of 100% would mean that the person would definitely end the relationship, whereas a score of 50% meant that they were as likely to end it as not. During the study, the participants were also rated by the researchers for their levels of physical attractiveness and given an overall 'mate value' score.

Shackelford found, unsurprisingly, that the more serious the infidelity, the greater the probability the person said they would divorce their partner. However, he also established that the more physically attractive women with higher 'mate values' were more likely to say they would divorce over lesser offences than the less attractive women. For men, the most important variable was if the woman had been unfaithful before: under these conditions, any second evidence of infidelity at any level would lead to divorce.

Shackelford's study offers an ingenious way of examining the role of infidelity avoiding some of the more serious ethical issues (although it does have its own issues, notably the rating of participants for their 'mate value'!). It also demonstrates that decisions to end relationships do not exist in a social vacuum: consistent with exchange approaches, the existence of attractive alternatives influences how much people are prepared to put up with. Of course, what people say they would do, and how they really react may be rather different!

Infidelity does not always lead to the end of a relationship. The way in which it is discovered may play an important part in whether or not couples split up, as observation of celebrity couples so often demonstrates. Afifo, Falato and Weiner (2001) studied 115 university students who had discovered that their partner was cheating on them. Afifo et al. asked each participant to recall how they had found out about the affair. Their answers fell into four main types of discovery:

- They were told by a third party
- They caught their partner 'red handed'
- They asked the partner outright
- The partner confessed without being asked.

Afifo et al. also asked the students to reflect on what happened to the relationship, whether they forgave their partner or split up. Unsurprisingly, they found that the method of discovery was strongly related to the relationship outcome. Those who had been told by a third party or caught the partner red handed were more likely to split up. Those whose partners had confessed were more likely to forgive them or renegotiate the relationship.

The dyadic level – communication and conflict

As we noted in Chapter 5, Regulating relationships, Gottman and Levenson (1992) found that four communication factors appeared to distinguish unhappy couples and these were strongly related to relationship dissatisfaction. These factors were criticism of the partner, contempt (scornfulness) for the partner, stonewalling (refusing to discuss issues) and defensiveness.

In a 2002 follow-up of the original couples using Love Lab methodology, Gottman examined the 21 couples who had subsequently divorced and looked back at their communication patterns using video-recorded evidence. He identified two specific patterns of communication in the divorced couples that were different to the 'staying together couples'. These were:

1 'Unregulated volatile positive and negative affect' – this communication pattern involved high levels of anger directed at the partner with arguments escalating negatively.

2 A 'neutral affective style' – this communication pattern was devitalized and bored. The partners seemed apathetic and showed little evidence of interest in their partner or affection towards them.

Gottman found that the first communication pattern was associated with early divorce in his sample. Couples showing this pattern were most likely to split up within the first seven years of marriage, showing the 'seven year itch' in action. Effectively, this form of negative communication appears to be so unpleasant for those involved that the relationship ends fairly quickly. This level of conflict is also apparent to others such as children, relatives and friends, which may play a part in the decision to end the relationship. However, couples who showed the second communication pattern tended to stay together for longer. These were more likely to divorce later on in the marriage, often when they were in their mid-forties or when they had teenage children.

Gottman has used these findings to develop the **two factor model** of relationship dissolution which predicts when rather than why couples will split up. His study goes a good way to explaining the patterns of divorce which show that two patches within a relationship are particularly vulnerable – the 'seven year itch' and the midlife of the relationship.

Research study → **A two factor model for predicting when a couple will divorce: Exploratory analyses using 14 year longitudinal data** (John Gottman, 2002)

In this longitudinal North American study lasting 14 years, 197 couples were originally recruited in 1983. Each member of the couple was assessed to measure their satisfaction with the relationship using two scales designed to measure marital satisfaction (Time 1). Of this sample, a total of 85 couples were selected for further study: this second sample consisted of a range of couples across the whole happiness/satisfaction spectrum. This group were then studied again four years later (Time 2) and then again every year for the next ten years. A total of 21 of these couples went on to divorce.

Gottman used a range of methods to study the communication patterns in couples. The Oral History method involved a semi-structured interview with the couple together in their own homes in which the couple were asked open-ended questions about how they had met, what their dating had been like, the good and the bad times in their relationship. The Interaction session took place in the lab: couples were asked to arrive at the lab separately after at least 8 hours apart (that is, after a working day) and then took part in three 15-minute discussions focusing on how their day had been, a problem in their relationship and a happy topic. While this discussion took place, the couple were recorded on hidden cameras and various aspects of their physiological functioning were measured.

Data was coded using a range of methods. Oral histories were coded for fondness, negativity and disappointment. The videotapes were coded for facial expressions of emotion using a scale devised by Ekman and Friesen (1978) and the speech was coded as either neutral, negative (that is, anger/whining) or positive (affection/interest). Coders were trained and showed high levels of inter-rater reliability.

Gottman found evidence for two factors that predicted divorce. Couples who divorced early on in their relationship showed higher levels of volatile, positive and negative communication. In contrast, couples who divorced later on in their relationship had a 'neutral affective style' – they showed little emotion and seemed switched off from each other. Those who went on to divorce showed a pattern of recasting the story of their relationship in a negative way.

👁 Breakdown of same-sex relationships

Many of the studies we have considered so far have examined breaking up of heterosexual relationships. As we noted in Chapter 1, there has been a tendency in the past to overlook differences and to assume that heterosexual models and norms could be applied to same-sex relationships. A major difference relating to the experience of relationship breakdown in same-sex couples relates to the lack of family support for couples when their relationship runs into difficulties. Becker (1988) found that compared to heterosexual couples, same-sex couples received much less by way of support or practical help when relationships ran into difficulties.

Another area where there are clear differences from heterosexual couples relates to the impact of infidelity. In many gay relationships, infidelity (sometimes referred to Extra Sexual Dyadic Activity or ESDA) is not viewed as 'cheating'. Instead, many gay couples have open relationships where ESDA is not just put up with, but is discussed, accepted and may even be welcomed. Hickson, Davies, Hunt and Weatherburn (1992) found that 56% of partnered gay men living in London were in an open relationship compared with 43% who abided by rules of monogamy. Forssell (2005) studied 110 male couples aged between 19 and 66 (mean age 35.7) living across North America. These included those with open relationships (non-exclusive) and those with more traditional closed (exclusive) relationships. They completed measurements of relationship adjustment and satisfaction as well as details of their sexual activities. Forssell found that communication (talking) about ESDA was associated with lower depression, better happiness and adjustment in relationships.

Forssell's study demonstrates the need to understand the unique norms and rules that apply to same-sex relationships, rather than imposing heterosexual models and rules which fit them poorly. This point is also demonstrated by Fitzgerald (2004) who has found that lesbians often continue to stay close friends after their relationship ends, unlike most heterosexual couples. Slavin (2009) argues that we need to acknowledge and accept that gay relationships have different rules and are organized in different ways to heterosexual relationships. We should not apply 'hetero-normative models' to them.

However, Gottman's findings relating to *communication patterns* appear to be equally as useful in predicting which same-sex relationships will break down. In 2003, Gottman et al. reported the results of an identical longitudinal study using Love Lab methodology, with a sample of same-sex couples. Gottman found that the same framework applied to same-sex couples: those who showed communication pattern 1 (unregulated volatile negative affect) split up after around seven years whereas those showing pattern 2 (a neutral affective style) split up later in the relationship. In a similar longitudinal study of gay couples, Kurdek (1992) found that those who split up were more likely than those who stayed together to show patterns of 'negative affect' – or arguing!

◉ How do relationships end?

As we said earlier, generalizations about relationship endings almost inevitably ignore the unique experiences of individuals. Some short-term relationships may simply 'fizzle out' or fail to get off the ground. Others may involve argument, discussion and negotiation. Hill, Rubin and Peplau (1976) carried out a series of interviews with the students in their sample who had split up. These revealed important points about timing: many people who were dissatisfied with their relationship used natural breaks in the college year (such as the end of term or summer holiday) to bring an unsatisfactory relationship to a relatively painless end. In this way, short-term relationships may end in a similar way to friendships: we just stop 'doing' the relationship, don't ring or meet up when we say we will, allowing the relationship to fizzle out.

Generally, where a couple do not live together, have shared property or children, there are likely to be fewer **barriers to dissolution** and it may be practically easier to disentangle from the relationship. However, this does not mean that the experience is necessarily less painful: emotional pain and trauma can occur in both short- and long-term endings, making it rather artificial to draw a clear distinction based on length of relationship.

Stage models of relationship breakdown

When two people have spent time together, invested in the relationship and developed interdependence in different areas of their life, the decision to end the relationship is unlikely to be taken lightly. Lee (1984) and Duck (1984) have both developed models that attempt to 'map out' the processes involved in breakdown in a series of stages.

Steve Duck (1984) conceptualizes the process of splitting up as a series of phases in which different things happen at different times. Duck offers an explanation as to why a couple may move from one phase into the next, arguing that one partner in the relationship reaches a *threshold* or a decision point which moves the process on to the next phase. These thresholds can be seen as tipping points that make/force changes in the relationship in one form or another and move the dialogue between the partners onwards.

The intra psychic phase – being unhappy

The start of the break-up process is when one of the members of the couple realize they are unhappy or seriously dissatisfied with some aspect of the relationship. At this point, they are likely to keep this to themselves although they may talk to their close friends about the relationship. The focus at this point is usually on the partner's inadequate behaviour of some sort: for example, they may feel that the amount of effort put into family and children is inadequate and their partner goes out and leaves them at home too much. The dissatisfaction is not aired to the partner at this point: in fact, many people may exist in this 'phase' for a long period, unhappy but unwilling to move forward and press for changes in the relationship, especially if they have invested a great deal. If the dissatisfaction builds up to such a point that the individual feels unable to carry on they will express this to their partner, moving into the next phase.

- *Threshold – I can't stand it anymore.*

The dyadic phase

Once one person has expressed their unhappiness with the relationship, the issue is now out in the open air. It may be that their partner is unhappy too and has their own grievances ('Well, you never want to go out any more'). The couple may argue, defend their own behaviour and engage in 'our relationship' talks about possible changes which might resolve the difficulties. They may also seek help in the form of professional couple counselling from organizations such as Relate. At this stage, the relationship can be saved if the partners are able to negotiate, communicate and resolve the conflict. However, if the causes of dissatisfaction fail to be resolved, one or both partners may eventually reach the next threshold where they feel that ending the relationship might be better than carrying on.

- *Threshold – I'd be justified in leaving.*

The social phase

In the social phase, the relationship problems become public. Both members of the couple tell chosen friends and family about the difficulties they are having and possibility of them splitting up. They are likely to tell their own version of what has happened to enlist support and to try getting people onto their side. They may also ask for advice about ways forward, for support or practical help. Family and friends may respond to this in different ways, for example offering support to help the couple stay together or advising them to split up. At this point, the break-up is becoming more and more likely although the relationship may still possibly be saved. The final threshold is reached when one partner moves the situation forward by taking some sort of action.

- *Threshold – I mean it.*

The grave dressing phase

The last phase of Duck's model takes place after the couple have announced the split and continues after they have separated. In this phase, which is really getting over the relationship, both parties try to get their side of the story across to people who matter to them. The reason for this is so that they can emerge with some social credibility in order to engage in future relationships. This phase is called 'grave dressing' as Duck believed that people needed to provide some account as to why their relationship died and to 'bury' it properly in order to move on. These versions are usually 'face saving' with the aim of showing other people that the break-up was not their fault but was justifiable. It is very rare that you hear people say 'I went out with him because he had a lovely car and loads of money and when he lost his job, I didn't get nice presents any more ...'!

A very similar model of relationship breakdown has been put forward by Lee (1984). According to Lee, the first stage of relationship difficulties is the realization of *dissatisfaction* by one or both partners. This dissatisfaction is *exposed* or brought out into the open. If one or both partners are interested in saving/continuing the relationship, the couple may discuss their problems (*negotiation*) to see if they can be resolved. If the couple are able to sort out their differences, the *resolution* stage may be successful in saving the relationship: if not, this will lead to the ending or *termination* of the relationship.

Commentary

As you can see, there is substantial overlap between these models with both Duck and Lee agreeing that breakdown starts with dissatisfaction and involves times of negotiation where the couple are focused on trying to mend their relationship. Both models apply specifically to relationships that have involved some degree of commitment. It is unlikely that a very short-term or superficial relationship would pass through these stages: in fact, a short-term relationship may be ended abruptly with little discussion or negotiation, sometimes by a change of Facebook status or a text message.

These are models of relationship maintenance and repair as well as breakdown. As we have noted previously, the processes of repair, maintenance and breakdown are intrinsically linked and can only be separated via their outcome. If a couple are able to negotiate and communicate, and if they have commitment to the relationship, then problems may be sorted out. This can happen at any point during the first two phases of Duck's model where many couples go on to sort out their differences and reorganize their relationship with new rules.

Duck's model provides us with a useful framework to conceptualize the rather messy ending of relationships. It is consistent with the cognitive–social perspective as it focuses predominantly on cognitive activity – what the two people in the relationship think.

However, the models have differences as well as similarities. Lee's model chooses to focus explicitly on the couple throughout. In contrast, Duck considers how friends, family and the wider social network may become involved in relationship breakdown in the 'social' phase. While Lee's model considers what happens until the relationship ends, Duck also focuses on the aftermath in the grave dressing stage.

Since its original inception, Duck has commented on the use of phase models to conceptualize relationship breakdown. He argues that models have conceptualized break-ups as existing separately from other aspects of human lives and have been seen largely in a social vacuum. This critique relates to the point we made at the start of this chapter, that the role of friends, family and social networks are, as yet, largely overlooked in relationship research. Duck and Rollie (2006) argue that we need to consider break-ups as part of the general changes and continuities that characterize human life. After all, the ending of one relationship is often the start of another!

Chapter summary

- Short-term relationships end every day. Long-term relationships end via divorce or legal separation
- Two periods in a relationship are most vulnerable to divorce, after seven years and in the midlife of the relationship
- Most short-term splits are one-sided. Some studies show gender differences in reasons for splitting up
- Individual factors such as marriage at an early age and attachment style influence later relationship breakdown
- Parental divorce has different effects on later relationships depending on how well it is resolved

- The importance of infidelity in splitting up is difficult to investigate and poses ethical issues. There is wide difference in tolerance of infidelity and it is often accepted in open, gay relationships
- Two communication factors predict later divorce: unregulated negative affect and a neutral affective style
- The first is associated with splitting up after about seven years. Those showing the second pattern are more likely to split up later in the relationship
- Phase models argue that couples move through different stages and reach thresholds that trigger changes in relationships
- Phase models have been criticized for seeing relationship breakdown in a social vacuum and ignoring the role played by family and friends

Further reading

Duck, S. (1992) *Human Relationships* (2nd edn, London: Sage) covers research into relationship breakdown and Duck's model in Chapter 3 in detail.

Chapter 7

Cultural variations in relationships

👁 Introduction

You may have already noticed that the research we have covered in the previous chapters has predominantly been carried out in a relatively small area of the western, economically developed world – North America, Australia and Northern Europe. In western societies such as these, relationships are based on a number of assumptions which many people take for granted. These are that individuals are relatively free to go out with different people, can choose to live together or marry and that a relationship can be ended by separation or divorce if it no longer meets the needs of the two people involved. Most of the theories we have examined so far, such as Kerckhoff and Davis's filter theory, the economic theories of relationship maintenance and Gottman's two factor model have been based on these assumptions.

However, these assumptions are not shared universally and are held in few places across the world. In many countries and in some religious groups such as Muslims and Hindus, parents and family members play a major part in the choice of partner, often arranging marriages for their offspring. **Arranged marriages** were common in the past in the United Kingdom and they remain the most common forms of marital arrangement across the globe today (Ingoldsby, 1995). As recently as 1993, one in four marriages in Japan, a modern industrial country, were arranged (Iwao, 1993). In this chapter we will explore how relationships are formed, conducted and organized in other parts of the world to the west.

As well as exploring differences between cultures, we will also consider the variations in relationships within cultures.

This chapter will cover:
- The important role played by culture in personal relationships
- Different types of cultures
- An evolutionary perspective on culture and mate preferences
- The formation of relationships through arranged marriages in traditional, modernizing and western cultures
- Happiness, love and satisfaction in arranged marriages
- Cross-cultural variations in relationship breakdown and divorce
- Variations in relationships within cultures

⊙ A cross-cultural approach to personal relationships

As we noted in Chapter 1, much of the early research into personal relationships took place in the 'academic power blocks' of North America and Western Europe. Findings of these studies were used to devise models of relationships that were then assumed to apply fairly universally. However, the emergence of cross-cultural social psychology in the 1970s demonstrated substantial variations in social behaviour and relationships in particular which challenged the assumption that relationships were conducted in similar ways across cultures.

What do we mean by 'culture'?

Although the word **culture** is widely used in daily language, it is difficult to define precisely and it is used in many different ways in different contexts, leading Hogg and Vaughan (2005: 614) to refer to it as 'a pervasive but slippery concept'. As far back as 1952, Kroeber and Kluckhohn noted over 150 different usages of the term. In common usage, cultural differences generally refer to any differences between one group of people and another. Some obvious cultural differences include ethnic background and religion.

Unpicking the idea of culture, Triandis et al. (1980) distinguished between two interrelated elements:

- *Objective aspects of culture:* these are physical entities which can be seen or heard. Examples of objective aspects of culture include clothing (such as wearing a veil) food, music and buildings such as a mosque or temple.

- *Subjective aspects of culture:* these are things that can't be seen in physical terms but exist within people's heads, such as beliefs, values and shared ideas. Subjective aspects of culture exert powerful and subtle influences on behaviour.

D'Ardenne and Mahtani (1990: 4) incorporate both of these aspects in their definition of culture as 'the shared history, practise, beliefs and values of a racial, regional or religious group of people'. Cultural beliefs and practices are not transmitted genetically but are passed from generation to generation through learning and teaching. Some of this may be explicit (as when children are instructed in religious practices) whereas other aspects are passed on implicitly. Children grow up accepting some things to be 'normal' or true, only to discover that other groups of people may do things in very different ways and have different beliefs.

How do cultures vary?

In order to simplify the complexity of cultural variation, cross-cultural psychologists have classified countries by using different dimensions. Hofstede (1980) presented a four-dimensional model that has been extremely influential in helping us to understand how cultures vary. In order to construct his model, Hofstede analysed questionnaires completed by 117,000 managers working for a multinational company (IBM) across 40 different countries using a statistical technique called factor analysis. He isolated four key dimensions relating to the attitudes and values held within the cultures:

1 *Masculinity/femininity* – Cultures can be divided in terms of the attributes they value. Some value traditionally masculine attributes such as achievement, independence and competition whereas others value feminine qualities such as cooperation. Japan scores highly on masculinity whereas Sweden and Denmark value feminine qualities. The UK is a broadly masculine culture.

2 *Power distance* – This dimension refers to whether relationships are broadly hierarchical or equal. Central and Southern American countries (for example Venezuela) score highly on power distance, and the most egalitarian/equal countries include Denmark and

Israel. The UK is relatively lower on power distance and is therefore classed as an egalitarian culture.

3 *Uncertainty avoidance* – This dimension refers to attitudes towards uncertainty and risk taking within a culture. Greece, Portugal and Japan score highly on avoiding uncertainties meaning that risk taking is broadly disapproved of whereas Denmark receives a low score.

4 *Individualism/collectivism* – This dimension refers to the importance placed upon personal choices such as marriage. In **individualistic cultures**, these choices are largely made by the individual, whereas the wider social group such as the family have much more influence in **collectivist cultures**. Southern American and many Asian countries such as Pakistan, Taiwan and Thailand are highly collectivist. The UK and USA are strongly individualistic.

This outline of Hofstede's model has demonstrated how complex cultural variations are. A simplified version of classifying cultures has been put forward by Fiske, Kitayama, Marcus and Nesbitt (1998) based on two of Hofstede's dimensions, individualism–collectivism and power distance. Fiske et al. suggest that:

- Western European nations (for example UK, France) are egalitarian and individualistic
- Eastern European nations (for example Slovakia, Greece) are hierarchical and individualistic
- Asian nations are hierarchical and collectivist.

In much research, cultural complexity is oversimplified to comparisons between individualist and collectivist cultures (Hogg and Vaughan, 2005). In broad terms, individualistic cultures place a large emphasis on the pursuit of individual happiness. Relationships are unions between two people and are freely chosen, although family views may play a part. They can be ended relatively easily by separation or divorce. Relationships in individualistic cultures are often characterized as voluntary, temporary and individualistic (Moghaddam, Taylor and Wright, 1993).

In contrast, in collectivist cultures such as Pakistan, relationships are seen as unions between families rather than individuals. The family play a much larger role in the formation of relationships, often using systems of arranged marriages. Once formed, it may be very difficult to end a relationship through separation or divorce as this is seen as bringing shame on both families. Relationships in collectivist cultures are often categorized as obligatory, permanent and an alliance between families rather than two individuals (Moghaddam et al., 1993).

The challenges of cross-cultural social psychology

Goodwin (1999) identifies a number of important themes in cross-cultural research in relationships. The foremost of these is establishing how cultural systems, with their own ideas and beliefs, are internalized as social norms that influence how people behave in their relationships. This sounds deceptively straightforward, but is rather more complex. Culture is not a variable that exists in isolation. The norms absorbed from culture interact with a range of individual factors including age, class and personality, as people respond to and interpret norms differently. Therefore, relationships are not influenced solely by culture or by individual personality but these two factors working together.

Another important theme relates to social change. Over the past twenty years, many parts of the world including Eastern Europe and East Asia have undergone dramatic economic and political changes which have altered how people live their lives. These changes are often referred to under the blanket terms of modernization and westernization. Modernization usually refers to developments in health and education leading to reductions in family size and increases in educational opportunities. Westernization generally refers to the adoption of western and individualistic beliefs: these may include the importance of the pursuit of happiness, the importance of equality of women and minority groups and the rejection of the ideas of fatalism. Relationships exist and adapt within the context of the social changes taking place. The processes of westernization and modernization are leading to the merging of cultures, along with new cultural forms. The result of this is that many of the cultural differences in relationships that have been taken for granted are being challenged by rapid social transitions (Goodwin and Pillay, 2006).

Finally, we need to be aware that relationships do not just vary between cultures: there are also dramatic variations within cultures. For example, the relationship experiences and beliefs of a young man growing up in South London in 2010 are likely to be very different to those of a woman in her sixties from the same area.

⊙ An evolutionary perspective on relationships: the search for cultural universals

According to the evolutionary perspective, relationships are driven by the need for reproductive success for men and women. As we saw in Chapter 2, the evolutionary perspective draws attention to the qualities men and women seek in potential partners, suggesting that these preferences are largely 'inbuilt' and originated because they led to reproductive success in the past. The evolutionary perspective predicts that men will prefer younger partners who are physically attractive, as these features are strongly linked to fertility. In contrast, women will be likely to seek older males with resources, such as wealth. If these preferences are indeed inbuilt, then similar qualities will be seen as attractive/desirable across different cultures.

These claims were investigated by Buss (1989). Buss surveyed the qualities sought in partners by 4601 men and 5446 women living in 37 countries across the world. Each participant was asked about the desirable age to get married and the preferred age of partners. They were also asked to rate 18 qualities of partners such as ambition and physical attractiveness for importance. Buss's main findings are shown in Table 7.1.

Number of cultures/37	Quality
37	Men preferred younger women and women preferred older men
37	Men valued physical attractiveness in partners more than women did
36	Women valued good financial prospects in partners more than men did
29	Women valued ambition in partners more than men did
23	Men valued chastity (faithfulness) in partners more than women did

Table 7.1 Relationships in 37 countries (Buss, 1989)

Buss's study provides some evidence for cultural universals in mate preferences. In all 37 cultures, men desired a female partner who was younger and, in almost all cultures, women placed more emphasis on the wealth and resources of male partners. In a second study in 1990, Buss surveyed a sample of 9494 men and women in 33 different countries and found that collectivist cultures, such as China, India and Iran, placed a higher value on virginity in women than western countries.

Men's preference for youthful partners is reinforced in studies of tribal societies such as the Kipsigis of Southern Kenya. Here, men pay a sum of money called a **bride price** to the family of the woman they marry. A study of relative bride prices (Borgerhoff Mulder, 1988) demonstrates that men pay the highest price for very young, healthy women, especially if they are claimed to be virgins. This is because their reproductive value is high and they are likely to produce many children. Much lower bride prices are paid for older women, those with any form of disability or women who already have children, as their reproductive value is seen to be lower. Higher prices are also paid for plumper girls by the Kipsigis as they are more likely to remain fertile even when food supplies are short.

In Chapter 2 we noted how men are attracted to females with a waist–hip ratio (WHR) of around .7, a shape that is strongly linked to fertility. Researchers have examined if this preference holds true across different cultures. Singh and Luis (1995) found a similar WHR preference in Chinese-Indonesian students living in the USA. However, studies of traditional cultures have indicated that WHR is less important than body mass especially in places where food is scarce. Anderson, Crawford, Nadeau and Lindberg (1992) reported a study in which body shape preferences were examined in 54 different countries. The countries were divided into four categories on the basis of food supply. These categories were very reliable, moderately reliable, moderately unreliable and very unreliable. Anderson et al. found that a heavier female body was preferred in 71% of the countries where food was scarce with minimal preference for a slender shape. In contrast, 60% of countries with a very reliable food supply preferred a slender or moderate body in women.

This preference is so marked that in some parts of the world where food is scarce, young women are deliberately fattened up in order to make them marriageable. The Tuareg tribe of the Sahara Desert prefer women bordering on a size considered obese in western societies. Tuareg parents force-feed their young daughters with milk-rich diets to make them gain weight and increase their value (Randall, 1995). It would appear that preferences for body shapes are finely 'tuned' to the specific environment: in places where food is easily available such as the USA and UK, a slimmer female body is preferred but in regions where food is scarce (for example sub-Saharan Africa) a larger body shape is desired.

Buss's (1989) study also points to the importance of wealth and resources in women's choice of partners. This is most marked in societies where a man's wealth will dramatically increase the chance of offspring surviving. However, the same principles are also found in rapidly modernizing countries such as Hungary where women prefer men with the same or higher levels of education as themselves. Education, of course, is linked to potential income and it makes evolutionary sense for women to seek partners who are likely to provide resources and wealth. Even in highly developed countries such as Japan, women seek the 'Three H's' in male partners: height, high education and high salary.

What about psychological qualities? Goodwin and Tang (1991) compared the preferences of British and Hong Kong Chinese students for the qualities sought in friends and potential partners. Goodwin found that British students valued sensitivity and humour in potential partners, whereas Hong Kong Chinese students put a high value on money mindedness and creativity, qualities important for success in the rapidly changing society. Hatfield and Sprecher (1995) compared partner preferences in three countries, USA (individualistic) Japan (collectivist) and Russia, which scores moderately on individualism–collectivism. They found that similar psychological traits including kindness, a sense of humour and openness were sought across cultures, suggesting that these traits may be universally valued.

Together, these findings imply that evolutionary preferences continue to exert a strong influence on partner selection, especially in less economically developed areas where food supplies are short and resources are not guaranteed. In parts of the world where resources are more reliable, inbuilt preferences appear to have less effect – presumably as they have less impact on survival and reproduction.

Summary

- Culture refers to shared history, beliefs and practices of a racial, religious or regional group
- Hofstede argues that cultures differ on four sets of values. The most important distinction is between individualistic and collectivist cultures
- In individualistic cultures, relationships are freely chosen and can be ended
- In collectivist cultures, relationships are often organized by family and may be difficult to end
- Cross-cultural studies show that similar qualities are sought in partners across different cultures

- Across cultures, men seek youth and attractiveness in female partners whereas women put a high value on male earning potential and career prospects
- Some traditional cultures continue to practise economic arrangements in marriages
- Preferences for female body shape are sensitive to the specific features of the environment important for reproductive success
- Similar psychological qualities such as kindness and a sense of humour appear to be valued universally

◉ Formation of relationships in collectivist cultures

Although there may be similar views across cultures about the desirable qualities sought in partners, the ways in which relationships are formed vary considerably. Once of the most obvious distinctions is the arrangement of marriages in many collectivist cultures. Arranged marriages are common in South Asia, notably Pakistan, India, Bangladesh and Sri Lanka, and in Middle Eastern and African countries. They are also commonly practised by religious groups, including Hindus and Muslims living in western societies.

Why are arranged marriages so common? Goodwin (1999) identifies a number of advantages of arranged marriages. In economic terms, arranged marriages enable political and economic links to be made between families, which are important when resources are in short supply. In social terms, they allow family elders to keep control of younger family members and protect family reputations. Finally, arranged marriages tend to be stable. While voluntary marriages based on factors such as attraction, desire and love may 'fizzle out' and end in divorce, arranged marriages tend to be very long lasting.

Arranged marriages are also based on the idea that young people are unlikely to make a good choice of lifetime partner for themselves. Potential partners are identified by family members or professional matchmakers, sometimes known as well-wishers. The well-wisher will consult with the family/parents about the specific requirements. They are likely to discuss the importance of family background, education, career prospects and profession as well as personal qualities such as appearance, height, hair and eye colour. In India, they will also discuss specific requirements relating to the caste of potential candidates. The well-wisher will then identify a candidate or a range of several candidates who meet the criteria set by the family. The list of potential candidates is presented to the family of the bride or groom for their approval: it may also be presented to the person wishing to marry who is generally known as the 'agent' (Batabyal, 2001).

The precise details of arranged marriages vary considerably, depending on the specific cultural context and the demographic nature of the family. Qureshi (1991) identifies three broad types of arranged marriage:

- *Planned* (also known as traditional arranged marriages): here, parents plan the entire process. There may be very little discussion or option to refuse the parents' choice of partner.
- *Delegation:* here, children (usually males) explain what type of partner they would like to parents who then seek a partner who fits these criteria.
- *Joint venture:* both parents and children are active in the mate selection process.

Further to this, Batabyal (2001) distinguishes between a 'modern arranged marriage' where the agent may be free to turn down the candidate and an 'introduction only' arranged marriage where the young couple are introduced and then left to pursue and develop the relationship themselves. Of course, the latter approach involves similar risks to those involved in voluntary relationships: the relationship may end at any time, leaving the individual with the pain and stigma of rejection.

Traditional arranged marriages

Traditional arranged marriages are most common in rural areas and in families who have lower levels of education (Zaida and Shuraydi, 2002). In traditional arranged marriages, the couple are unlikely to have met much before the marriage and may have only seen photos of each other. Brides are often very young when married. In some rural areas, an arranged marriage may be welcomed by young women as an escape from family controls and constraints, allowing them greater freedom than the parental home. Marriages are arranged taking into account economics, social status and family reputation (Goodwin, 1999).

Economics play a very important part in arranged marriages. Parents seek partners who they perceive to be a good match in financial terms and arranged marriages often take place within a context of financial negotiation. Two long-standing economic practices are the *bride price* system and the *dowry*. A bride price is a sum of money paid by the parents of the groom to the bride's family to compensate them for their loss of services from their daughter. The bride price system is common in Africa and continues to be valued even as the country undergoes economic and social change. In a study of graduate students from South African universities, 88% of the sample were in favour of the system (Mwamwenda and Monyooe, 1997). In Europe, the Roma ethnic group living mainly in Bulgaria continue the practice of the bride price. Pamparov (2007) argues that the function of the bride price is to ensure that any children from the marriage will be kept by the groom's family if the marriage breaks down: it is also useful in protecting the bride from maltreatment. The average price paid by one Roma group is around 2500 Euros, making this a substantial investment.

Dowries are sums of money or gifts for the home, given by the bride's family to the couple to 'set up' the household. A large dowry may act as a financial inducement to encourage suitable partners. The practice of giving dowries was commonplace in the UK until the end of the nineteenth century. Despite being made illegal in India through the Dowry Prohibition Act (1961), the practice continues to grow in India. Srinivasan and Lee (2004) investigated women's attitudes to the dowry system in Bihar, a northern province of India and found almost two-thirds of the 4000-plus women sampled disapproved of the dowry system.

As marriages are viewed as alliances between families, the social standing of the family is important in the choice of an arranged marriage. Arranged marriages in Iran and traditional African societies often involve inter-marrying between cousins. A study in Kuwait (Al-Thakeb, 1985) found that over half of arranged marriages involved relatives, generally first cousins.

Arranged marriages in modernizing cultures

In rapidly modernizing countries such as Turkey, India and China, young people are increasingly in contact with westernized ideas of free choice and wish to have more say over their choice of partner. While many families still opt for traditional arranged marriages, others have modified their views to allow a modern arranged/joint venture marriage. Families with higher levels of education and those living in urban areas are most likely to have changed their practices (Zaida and Shuraydi, 2002). Some families may even offer young people the choice between an arranged or a love marriage. Young men are more likely than women to voice their desire to take an active part in choosing a partner, demonstrating how traditional ideas of gender socialization continue to affect marriage practices.

Sprecher and Chandak (1992) examined the attitudes towards arranged versus love marriages in 66 young people in India and found that they saw advantages and disadvantages to both systems. Arranged marriages were seen as valuable in bringing family approval but risky in terms of not knowing the partner very well. Love marriages and the dating system were viewed positively in terms of having fun but also were seen as potentially risky as the relationship may end without marriage. Similarly, Umadevi, Venkataramaiah and Srinivasulu (1992) studied a sample of 180 female Indian university students from both professional and non-professional backgrounds, comparing their preferences for arranged or love marriages. They found that both groups of women were happy with the idea of an arranged marriage if it was organized with the consent of the two young people involved. They were also comfortable with the idea of love marriages if parents approved of the choice. These studies demonstrate the importance placed on the approval of the family for marriage partners in modern India. An arranged marriage may also be viewed as a 'fall back' position or an option to return to if the young person doesn't find a partner on their own.

Arranged marriages in western cultures

As well as being commonplace in traditional collectivist cultures, arranged marriages also take place in western societies. Many religious groups such as Muslims and Hindus continue with traditional practices after migrating to western countries. Second and third generation migrants in the UK and USA grow up surrounded by the views of dominant western culture which views choice of marriage partner as normal, desirable and essential for happiness. Despite the adoption of western ideas by younger people, arranged marriages continue to be seen as desirable by many parents. Ghuman (1994) studied British and Canadian Sikhs, Hindus and Muslims and found arranged marriages were still common practice. However, there were considerable variations between the three religious groups. Sikh and Hindu families had modified their practice from traditional arranged marriages to some degree of delegation: they were likely to allow a young couple to meet and get to know each other socially and to play some part in the decision-making process. Goodwin et al. (1997) studied 70 Gujerati Hindu couples living in Leicester and found that less than 10% had traditional fully arranged marriages, with most having a large element of choice involved. These studies demonstrate how western ideas are gradually modifying traditional arranged marriages into more westernized forms.

However, in Ghuman's 1994 study, most British and Canadian Muslim families continued the practice of traditional arranged marriages with little discussion between parents and offspring. Not surprisingly, young Muslims were the most likely to rebel against arranged marriages of all three religious groups. In all groups, the issue of arranged marriages caused inter-generational conflict between parents and their offspring.

The process of internalizing the views of a different culture is known as **acculturation** (Hogg and Vaughan, 2005: 636). Young people exposed to opposing sets of marital practices from the home and dominant culture, are likely to experience **acculturative stress**, an uncomfortable state arising from the clashes between cultures. Zaida and Shuraydi (2002) have investigated the feelings of young Muslim women about arranged marriages using qualitative research methods which have enabled them to capture their participants' views and experiences in rich detail.

Qualitative research study → Perceptions of arranged marriages by young Pakistani women living in a western society (Zaidi and Shuraydi, 2002)

This qualitative study was carried out in Canada and the USA to investigate the perceptions and views of arranged marriages in a group of second generation, Pakistani, Muslim women. Both researchers were also Muslim women of Pakistani origin. The researchers sampled 20 single women aged between 16 and 30 using unstructured interviews. This interview method enabled them to re-order and re-phrase questions as necessary and to generate rich and detailed data about the beliefs and feelings of young women towards arranged marriage.

Data was then analysed using a qualitative method called Interpretive Interactionism. Researchers transcribed (wrote out) the interviews then looked for commonalities and themes/patterns emerging from the data. In order to do this it was important for the researchers to put aside their own views, so as not to 'contaminate' the data: this is an important principle in qualitative research.

Five key themes emerged from the transcribed interviews:

- *Attitudes to romantic love:* for three-quarters of the sample, love was seen as essential for marriage
- *Preferred method of partner selection:* most of the women were strongly in favour of choice rather than arranged marriages
- *Redefining arranged marriages:* most of the women preferred the method of joint venture. Even those in favour of arranged marriages wanted to meet their prospective husband first and get to know them
- *Reasons for engaging in arranged marriages:* most of the women felt that only extreme situations – such as serious illness of a parent – would lead them to consider complying with an arranged marriage
- *'Breaking the silence':* the desire to speak about their feelings

The researchers concluded that 'growing up in western society is an agonizing, stressful process for Muslim females'. In one of the participant's words, the situation was no win: 'Both cultures to me emphasizes the exact opposite things, which creates a rift in my thinking pattern.' Acculturative stress indeed!

Arrangement of marriages through dating sites

One approach used by an increasing number of young Asians in western cultures involves the use of marital dating websites. This approach stands somewhere between a completely free choice marriage and a traditional arranged marriage. Shaadi.com is a serious matrimonial website aimed at Asian people. Launched in 1997, by Anupam Mittal, Shaadi (which means marriage in Hindi) has attracted over 15 million users in its history. Today it has over 5 million active members and is rapidly growing with 6000 new profiles added every day. The owner of the site has claimed that over one million marriages have taken place in couples who met via Shaadi.com.

Why is this website so popular? Shaadi.com allows its members to make extremely specific searches for potential partners in a similar way to those employed by matchmakers or well-wishers in arranged marriages. Manzoor (2009) describes the ethos of Shaadi.com saying that 'finding an ideal partner is about creed and career rather than chemistry'. This reinforces the importance of similar backgrounds, beliefs and values in a relationship. The search criteria allow members to ask questions about family values, profession and interests, factors that are typically used by traditional matchmakers to find an appropriate partner. It is perfectly possible on Shaadi.com to search for a partner who is a doctor living around Birmingham, of medium height, who wishes to have a family and enjoys playing sports.

Supporters of the website argue that it puts power back into the hands of young Asians, allowing them some choice and autonomy over their search for a partner. At the same time, it allows them to conform to the traditional ideals of arranged marriages by seeking partners from specific families, backgrounds and professions. It can be seen as a halfway house between arranged marriages and freely chosen love marriages for young Asians living in individualistic western societies. Manzoor argues that marriage is 'harder for second-generation British Asians, burdened by their parents' expectations but looking for more than marriage to a stranger'.

Commentary

As we have seen, the term 'arranged marriage' is something of a catch-all for a varied and bewildering range of relationship options. Arranged marriages take place in different ways and with differing degrees of power/autonomy from the young people involved. These variations suggest that we should view marriage practices as existing on a sliding scale, with fully arranged marriages at one end and fully chosen love marriages at the other. Between the two extremes are marriages that are partly arranged and those in which family views and preferences play a large part. In an examination of 42 traditional hunter-gatherer societies, Harris (1995) found that only 6 gave young people a completely free choice over their marriage partner. In practice, there are few societies that exist at either end of the scale: almost all cultures have some limits set on who they can marry or have a relationship with (Goodwin, 1999).

In some cultures, the tradition of arranged marriage has been handed down through generations. Parents who decide on arranged marriages are very likely to have been married using the same process. The failure to arrange a marriage or the allowance of a love marriage may be seen as a failure on the part of the parents to maintain control over their children. In cultures where children are brought up with expectations of arranged marriage, they are less likely to challenge them. However, in rapidly modernizing cultures, where western ideas of love and choice are becoming adopted, young people may experience the stress of living between different cultural ideas. Zaidi and Shuraydi's study demon-

strates clearly the relationship dilemmas facing second and third generation migrants who are exposed to both cultural models of relationships.

Berry (1984) identified the dilemma facing immigrants as a choice
between maintaining the values of the home culture as against accepting
those of the new, host culture. These options include:

- Integration – keeping the values of the home culture, but relating to
  the dominant culture
- Assimilation – giving up the values of the home culture and taking
  on the views of the dominant culture
- Separation – keeping the home culture and refusing to integrate
  with the dominant culture
- Marginalization – giving up the home culture but failing to take on
  the values of the dominant culture.

Of these options, integration is likely to lead to least acculturative
stress, although the process of integration may take time (Hogg and
Vaughan, 2005). Young people may also develop dual or bicultural identi-
ties, defining themselves as British Asian, Hispanic American or Greek
Australian. This may enable new forms of relationships to be defined and
pursued, such as those using marital websites.

◉ Regulating arranged marriages

In western voluntary relationships, love is seen as a prerequisite for
marriage by most people. Ideas of love and metaphors in western culture
involve involuntary images: we 'fall' in love, are love struck by 'cupid's
arrow' and occasionally experience 'love at first sight'. These concepts sit
uneasily with arranged marriages. Here, couples meet with the explicit
idea of developing a lasting, loving relationship. Rather than love leading
to marriage, marriage leads to love, which is viewed as a quality that
develops as two people get to know each other. In arranged marriages
'learning to love' is the mechanism by which love develops rather than
'falling in love'. In an exploration of this, De Munck (1998) considered
how the ideas of romantic love can co-exist within a framework of
arranged marriages in Sri Lanka. He argues that, even where marriages
are arranged with little choice, ideas about romantic love still exist even
though they are often 'invisible from public view' and form the background rather than the foreground to the marriage.

Happiness and satisfaction

In Chapter 5, we considered how voluntary relationships are maintained and regulated by the people within them using economic ideas of investments and equity. These concepts appear to sit rather uneasily with arranged marriages where the option of ending the relationship through divorce may be very difficult or impossible.

Some studies have suggested that arranged marriages may be happier in the long term than love marriages. In a classic study, Gupta and Singh (1982) compared professional married couples living around Jaipur City, India: 25 couples had chosen their partners and were classed as love marriages, whereas the other 25 were arranged marriages. The couples were carefully matched: all were university graduates and lived within nuclear families. They had also been married for different intervals from one year to ten years or more.

Gupta and Singh asked each member of the couple to complete two scales, on how much they loved their partner and how much they liked their partner. They found that couples who had married for love had – unsurprisingly – much higher love scores than those with arranged marriages for the first five years of the marriage. However, love decreased for both men and women in love marriages but increased in arranged marriages. After five years, both men and women in arranged marriages loved their partners more than those who had originally married for love (see Figure 7.1)

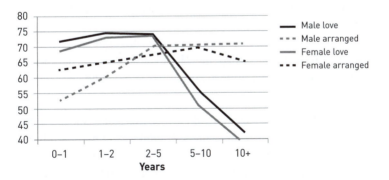

Figure 7.1 **Love scores in love marriages and arranged marriages**

A similar pattern was shown for the scores on liking: this started high in love marriages but decreased dramatically after about two years especially for men. In arranged marriages, liking started at a relatively low level but increased after two years so that arranged partners liked each other more than those who had married for love (see Figure 7.2).

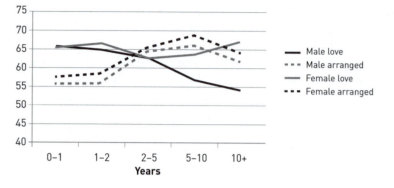

Figure 7.2 Liking in love marriages and arranged marriages

Gupta and Singh's study demonstrates the claim that love marriages start hot and grow cold, whereas arranged marriages start cold and grow hot. Other studies have confirmed these findings. Yelsma and Athappilly (1988) studied three types of couples: North American couples and Indian couples who had married for love, and Indian couples who were in arranged marriages. In all three groups, the partners were asked to complete questionnaires rating their relationships for communication and for satisfaction. The researchers found that the Indian couples with arranged marriages were happier and had higher satisfaction than either group of love marriages.

Why have arranged marriages been traditionally high in satisfaction and stability? Yelsma and Athappilly (1988) argue that a number of factors lead to high satisfaction in arranged marriages. The most important of these appear to be:

- The careful selection/matching of partners for education and social background. As we noted in Chapter 4, similarity of many kinds is associated with happier and longer lasting relationships
- The considerable support given to the couple from family on both sides (for example help with childrearing). As separation and divorce are viewed negatively, family and social support networks are likely to provide more emotional and practical help to the couple when things become difficult.

The studies described above took place over twenty years ago, before the forces of westernization had begun to impact on India. More recent studies of arranged marriages in India and China have shown a less clear picture. Myers, Madathil and Tingle (2005) compared 45 couples in arranged marriages in India with 45 US couples in love marriages. They found no difference in overall happiness and satisfaction between the two types, suggesting that arranged marriages remain as happy/ successful despite social changes. However, a study carried out in China by Xioahe and Whyte (1990) found that women in love marriages were happier and more satisfied than those in arranged marriages, implying that social changes and western expectations may have already influenced expectations in China. Furthermore, the traditionally low divorce rates in collectivist cultures are beginning to rise. These findings show the importance of contextualizing research within the pattern of social changes taking place.

Dealing with conflict

What happens when arranged marriages run into difficulties and problems? The phase models presented by Duck (1984) and Lee (1984) take the view that negotiations are carried out within the context of partners being able to leave the relationship. One area that is relatively under-studied is the regulation of arranged marriages and the methods used by couples to negotiate and resolve conflict in cultures where divorce is frowned upon. The research study carried out by Goodwin et al. (1997) of 70 British Asian couples explored how they dealt with emotional problems and marital difficulties. The researchers found that couples preferred to solve problems between themselves. Over half the couples said they would not involve anyone else in their difficulties as this may lead to tension in the wider family. Family help was more likely to be sought if the problem was minor, in which case a same-sex blood relative (such as an auntie for the wife or uncle for the husband) could be enlisted. Guru (2009) argues that divorce and marital breakdown, while apparently rising in Asian British couples, remains 'invisible and neglected' in the research literature.

Relationship breakdown

As we noted in Chapter 6, divorce and relationship breakdown have become increasingly common in industrialized, western societies in the past thirty years, currently standing at around 40% of all marriages. In most western countries, unhappiness with the partner is seen as a justifiable reason to end the relationship and seek happiness with someone else. Traditionally, collectivist cultures have shown a very different pattern with few relationships ending in divorce even though it is technically available in most countries of the world. In China, for example, the divorce rate was just under 4% until fairly recently (Xioahe and Whyte, 1990) and in India the proportion of marriages ending in divorce has hovered around 1.1%.

Reasons for divorce

There is fairly wide agreement in the main grounds for divorce across cultures. Betzig (1989) studied the reasons given for divorces across 160 different societies. She found the most common reasons given were:

- Infidelity: Consistent with evolutionary explanations, this was most likely to end a marriage when the female partner was unfaithful rather than the male
- Infertility: Inability for a couple to have children together
- Cruelty or maltreatment: generally by the male partner of his wife.

Here we will examine some of the aspects of collectivist cultures that are likely to contribute to the low divorce rates. We will also consider how social changes such as westernization may contribute to rising divorce rates in collectivist cultures.

Factors influencing divorce rates

One of the main factors influencing divorce rates is how difficult it is to end a relationship in terms of social acceptability. While it is relatively easy to gain a divorce and start a new relationship in the west, this is much more difficult in collectivist cultures where there are strong barriers to relationship dissolution. Johnson (1998) argues that structural forces such as cultural pressures to stay together along with moral obligations have been underestimated in western accounts of relationship breakdown, which have focused fairly exclusively on personal feelings.

In China, marriage is seen as 'a socially serious event' (Goodwin, 1999: 84) which is not to be undertaken lightly. Permission to divorce from employers or community committees was needed until recently. Ending a marriage through divorce leads to severe consequences for a couple and for their children. They are likely to face rejection by relatives, being turned out of the family and personal pain of loss of face. Unlike western society, it is difficult to find another partner and embark on a new relationship. Housing may also be difficult to find when a couple separate. In Saudi Arabia, a man may divorce his wife without giving a reason: in contrast, a woman may only divorce her husband if she has specifically made provision in her marriage contract to do this. In addition, women in Saudi Arabia face severe penalties from divorce. The father is given custody of any children of the marriage and the disgraced wife is sent back to live with her parents. It's probably not surprising that there are few takers, even though divorce is technically available!

Another influential factor is religion. In many faiths, marriage is viewed as a contract with God which should not be broken at the whim of the people involved. European countries, including Ireland, Poland and Italy, where many of the population follow the Roman Catholic faith have traditionally had very low divorce rates. Alongside religion, traditional beliefs may also play a part in the reluctance to divorce. Many people in China believe in a concept called 'Yuan' an idea taken from Buddhism, which loosely translates as being fated to be together. A traditional Chinese proverb goes something like this:

If you have *Yuan* for each other, though you are thousands of miles apart, you will still meet. If you don't have *Yuan* even if you are face to face, you will never know each other. (Cited in Goodwin, 1999: 69)

Social changes: westernization and increasing divorce rates

As we noted at the start of this chapter, relationships do not occur in a vacuum but are intrinsically linked to other social changes taking place. This is especially true of divorce. Where societies are experiencing social changes such as economic modernization and changes to women's roles, divorce rates are rising. Iran has seen a rapid increase in divorce. Many couples rushed into marriage during the Islamic revolution, often for political reasons. This and the war with Iraq have both contributed to the rising divorce rate. Similarly, the divorce rate has begun to increase in China since it began the processes of westernization in the late 1970s. Divorce rates are now higher in arranged marriages than those who married for love (Whyte, 1990). Japan has also seen a recent increase in divorce rates to around 30% of marriages. This may be linked to factors such as increased female employment, which enables women to live independently (McKenry and Price, 1995). Alexy (2008) has studied the explanations and justifications given by couples for the ending of their marriages in Japan. He argues that couples largely use western ideas such as the need for self-fulfilment and the pursuit of happiness to justify ending marriages.

Summary

- Arranged marriages are common in collectivist cultures and in some religious groups
- There are different kinds of arranged marriage giving differing degrees of choice
- Traditional arranged marriages are based on economics and family reputation whereas modern arranged marriages give more choice/involvement
- In western cultures, the clash between the values of home culture and dominant culture often leads to inter-generational conflict and acculturative stress
- There are substantial inter-cultural variations in arranged marriages
- Arranged marriages in collectivist cultures report high levels of happiness and satisfaction
- Arranged marriages in modernizing cultures are associated with lower levels of happiness
- Although divorce is technically available in most places, rates have traditionally been low in collectivist cultures
- Common reasons for divorce include infidelity, infertility and cruelty
- Divorce rates are increasing in rapidly modernizing countries such as Japan and China as western ideas become more widespread

◉ Further reading

An excellent coverage of this area is given in *Personal Relationships Across Cultures*, Robin Goodwin (1999) published by Routledge.

Chapter 8

Effects of relationships

👁 Introduction

As we have seen in the preceding chapters, relationships occupy a good deal of time. They are incredibly important to most people's happiness and it is not surprising that they affect emotions and feelings. However, there is also a growing body of evidence suggesting that relationships have effects on physical health and the likelihood of developing illnesses of many kinds. Health psychologists have sought to establish the extent of these effects and most have no doubt that relationships influence both emotional and physical health in the short and long term. Goleman (2006) claims that 'good relationships act like vitamins whereas bad relationships act like poisons', a view reinforced by Smith and Mackie (2000: 443) who argue that the claim of relationships affecting our health is now 'beyond dispute'.

A variety of studies have demonstrated how the mere company of other people can lead us to feel less anxious in difficult situations – even when they are strangers. In one study, Kulik, Mahler and Moore (1996) looked at the recovery rate among people who had undergone serious heart surgery. They examined objective data including drug records, requests for pain relief and length of stay, and related these to factors such as sharing a room. Kulik et al. found that those who were 'paired up' with a post-operative roommate (who had already undergone surgery) spent more time talking about their fears and anxieties, but consequently requested fewer anti-anxiety drugs and sedatives before their own operations when compared with those who were paired with another pre-operative roommate. In simple terms, the experience of talking to another person who had undergone a similar procedure had a powerful physical effect on their ability to cope with the situation.

In this chapter, we will examine the evidence behind Goleman's claim and consider the effects of relationships on emotional well-being and physical health. As we will see, health psychologists have investigated the detrimental effects of unhappy relationships as well as the positive benefits offered by friends and lovers. A growing body of research over the past twenty-five years or so has begun to establish which bodily systems are affected by conflict in relationships. However, it has proved difficult to establish causal links in this area as most studies involve comparisons between naturally occurring groups (for example married, single and divorced people) with little control over variables making it difficult to establish the causes of observed differences.

This chapter will cover:

- Research methods and data types used in 'effects' research
- Epidemiological studies of physical and mental health
- Self-report measures of physical and mental health
- Explanations of the 'marriage benefit'
- The negative effects of relationship conflict on stress hormones and the cardiovascular and immune systems
- The positive effects of good relationships on mental and physical health
- The importance of social support in health and illness
- Explaining gender differences in effects research
- The benefits of pets on health and well-being

Thinking scientifically → **Different kinds of data**

As you read this introduction, you may have wondered how researchers investigate links between relationships and well-being. Gathering information on the effects of relationships poses a range of methodo-logical challenges for the psychologist. Firstly, researchers must decide which kinds of effects they are interested in. Different effects might include happiness, satisfaction, depression, suicide rates or even number of illnesses and life expectancy. While effects on emotional well-being may occur almost immediately, effects on phys-ical health may take a very long time to become apparent and research requires longitudinal studies and follow-up of participants over many years. There may also be difficulties in collecting representative samples. People with unhappy or troubled relationships are less likely to volunteer to take part, or may drop out of longitudinal studies.

Working from objective statistical data, researchers can look for associations between relationships and health, by examining how many illnesses people develop, (the **morbidity rate**), how long they live (**life expectancy**) or when they die (the **mortality rate**). By comparing statistics for different groups of people (for example those who are married, cohabiting, single, separated or divorced) we can gather measurements of a rather crude nature of the effects of relationships. Statistical studies of this nature are known as **epidemiology** and we will consider some of these below.

Epidemiological studies show us the differences in how long divorced, married or single people live but they do not explain why these differences/effects might occur. If we are interested in establishing the precise effects on bodily systems, then physiological measurements may be used. Researchers working within health psychology have typically examined a range of bodily systems such as the cardiovascular (heart), endocrine (hormone) and immune systems to see how different kinds of stress may impact upon these. A study of this nature might measure changes to blood pressure or heart rate during arguments between partners. You may be surprised to find that researchers have chosen to investigate a range of bodily responses to conflict, including dental health and sperm concentration and quality. This kind of bodily data is often referred to as **material data**.

Material data has a number of advantages: it is relatively free from deliberate participant reactivity. Most people are unaware of their body's responses such as blood pressure and are unable to consciously control them; meaning that data like this is relatively uncontaminated and free from demand characteristics. Someone might state that arguments with their partner do not bother them, but their heart rate or immune system may tell a very different story. Material data is also relatively easy to measure using objective measuring tools such as blood tests. Kiecolt-Glaser and Newton (2001: 487) argue that studies of this nature give us 'solid, mechanistic evidence of how marital functioning can have direct consequences for cardio vascular, endocrine and immune functioning'.

However, material data tells us very little about feelings or emotions. Our third type of data in this area uses *self-reports* gathered from questionnaires or interviews. These may involve self-completion scales in which individuals rate their own health, for example a symptom checklist of illnesses. They may involve complex question-naires with many items or simple scales consisting of one or two ques-tions such as 'Compared with other people your own age, how would you describe your health?' Emotional states such as happiness or depression may also be measured in similar ways. These reports lack the objectivity of material data and are prone to social desirability effects. However, they may offer an insider viewpoint into health and feelings which is unavailable using either of the other data types.

As you read this chapter, you will meet studies that have used these approaches. You may wish to think about how the choice of data is closely linked to the kind of research question or hypothesis the researcher wishes to test.

Epidemiological studies of physical health

Epidemiological studies examine statistics for patterns and differences in the physical and mental health of different groups of people. Typic-ally, they compare people who are married, divorced, cohabiting or single in terms how long they live (life expectancy), the illnesses they develop (the morbidity rate) and when they die (the mortality rate). Epidemiological studies show clear differences in life expectancy and mortality rates of married and non-married (single, divorced or sepa-rated) people. One example of this type of research study is the Charle-ston Heart Study (Sbarra and Nietert, 2009), which has been ongoing for over forty years. This study has examined a sample of around 1300 adults between 1960 and 2000, following them at regular intervals to establish life expectancy. The researchers found that those who were separated or divorced at the start of the study have the highest mortality rates and die at an earlier average age than all other groups. Being sepa-rated or divorced later in the study is also associated with a shorter lifespan. However, this risk appears to drop if/when divorced partici-pants remarry, leading the researchers to argue that it is the amount of time that people live as separated or divorced which is important to later health, rather than the simple fact of splitting up.

Epidemiological studies also demonstrate that permanent singleness is associated with poorer health and life expectancy for both sexes but has a greater health impact on men than women. Ross, Mirowsky and Golds-teen (1990) established that the mortality rate for single women was 50%

greater than married women whereas for men, the risk of being single led to 250% greater mortality rate compared to married men. In agreement with these figures, Angier (1990) found that unmarried men between the ages of 45 and 64 had twice the death rate of married men, even when smoking habits, drinking and obesity were taken into account.

Other studies have demonstrated that social isolation (loneliness) arising from a lack of intimate relationships is a major risk factor for morbidity and mortality. In fact, Kiecolt-Glaser and Newton (2001) argue that social isolation has as much of a negative effect on health as well-established factors such as smoking, obesity and high blood pressure.

◉ Epidemiological studies of mental health

Epidemiological studies of mental health compare rates of depression and anxiety in relation to marital status. Results of these studies have generated rather contradictory findings relating to men and women. In 1973, Gove and Tudor examined the proportion of women and men who developed common mental health problems such as depression. When Gove and Tudor examined groups with different marital statuses, they found that single and divorced men had higher rates of mental illnesses such as depression than those who were married. However, this pattern was reversed for women, as married women had higher rates of depression and anxiety than their single counterparts.

Gove and Tudor argued that these findings showed that marriage benefited men emotionally at the cost of women. They pointed to the role of marriage as the cause of women's greater mental distress. At the time, marriage often meant an end to employment for women outside the home. This and the frustration arising from the menial, unpaid 'housewife' role were seen to be prime causes of depression. For those women who did work outside the home, lack of equality in the workplace and poorly paid jobs were the norm. This interpretation became known as Gove's *sex-role theory of mental illness*.

Since 1972, Gove and Tudor's findings have been revisited by many researchers, with varying results. If Gove and Tudor's interpretation was correct, the dramatic changes in women's roles with increased opportunities for participation in higher education and employment should have altered the pattern of married women's distress seen in the original study. Many studies have supported this claim. Afifi, Cox and Ennis (2006) compared groups of single mothers, married mothers and divorced mothers and found the highest rates of depression were in the divorced group. Gutierrez-Lobos et al. (2000) compared the rates of depression in a large sample of Austrians living in Vienna and found that both men and women who had never married or who had divorced, had higher rates of depression than married men and women (see Table 8.1). However, despite these changes, Gove and Tudor's original findings still hold true: married women have more than twice the rate of depression than married men, suggesting they still benefit less emotionally from marriage.

	Men	Women
Married	30.9	72.2
Never married	97.9	131.9
Divorced	107.0	144.9
Widowed	51.1	59.3

Table 8.1 Rates of depression per 100,000 (Gutierrez-Lobos et al., 2000)

However, not all studies agree with this claim. A meta-analysis by Hall (2000) examined a series of studies comparing the emotional benefits of marriage to men and women. Results suggested that men's marital gains over women had declined significantly since Gove's study, and by 1990, ceased to exist at all. In fact, Hall's meta-analysis suggests that positions may have reversed recently so that women appear to benefit more from marriage today. For example, married women are one-third as likely to experience a substance-use disorder (alcohol dependency) as married men. There are a number of difficulties interpreting the results of these studies. One is that specific disorders such as depression or alcohol abuse tell different stories. Depression is more commonly diagnosed in women than men whereas alcohol abuse is more common in men. Another problem is that many epidemiological studies combine the data from currently single people in one category, comprising divorced, never married and widowed people.

Figures showing extreme mental distress indicated by suicide rates tell a similar story to the figures on physical health. Single people are at greater risk of suicide than those in relationships. Unmarried men have a higher risk of suicide than married men of all ages and in one American study (Stack, 1990) almost three times more single men aged 25–44 committed suicide than their married counterparts (see Figure 8.1).

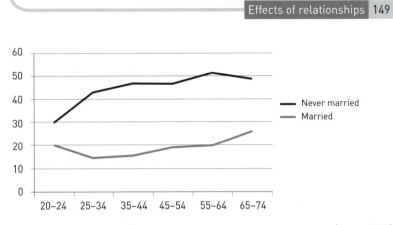

Figure 8.1 Suicide rates of American men per hundred thousand people (Stack, 1990)

A similar picture is shown with suicide rates of women (see Figure 8.2). Single women aged 25–34 have almost three times the suicide rate of their married counterparts. Based on American data, these figures indicate that people in relationships are less likely to experience extreme emotional distress leading to suicide.

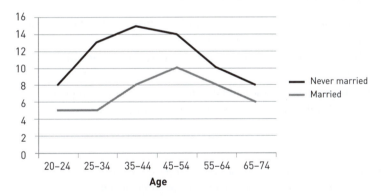

Figure 8.2 Suicide rates of American women per hundred thousand (Stack, 1990)

Self-report data and mental health

Self-report data is gathered from completion of questionnaires and scales. Studies using self-report measurements indicate, unsurprisingly, that relationship problems are associated with increased levels of psychological distress (Beach, Fincham and Katz, 1998) and depression is about ten times more common in men and women who are experiencing relationship difficulties. Many studies have demonstrated that unmarried people experience greater unhappiness and more symptoms of distress/ depression than those who are married. Separated and divorced people also report lower levels of happiness and well-being than those who are in stable relationships (Mastekaasa, 1995). The emotional benefits of secure, long-term relationships also apply – although to a slightly lesser extent – for cohabiting gay and lesbian couples. Wienke and Hill (2009) studied a group of 282 same-sex couples, comparing them with heterosexual married couples, cohabitees and singletons, and found that partnered gay people were happier than single people – both gay and straight – suggesting that the same relationship benefits apply to committed relationships regardless of sexual orientation. Similarly, Coyle (1993) has considered if the 'marriage benefit' appears in gay male couples. Coyle examined the psychological well-being (PWB) of 140 partnered gay men using a 30-item General Health Questionnaire (GHQ-30) and found that participants showed a level of well-being similar to single men from the general population and higher than that of divorced/separated and widowed men.

Three key themes emerge from these studies:

1 Permanent singleness and social isolation are associated with poorer mental health and shorter life expectancy.
2 The effects of singleness appear to be more detrimental to men's health than to women.
3 Relationship breakdown and divorce are associated with poorer physical and mental health for both women and men.

Summary

- Epidemiological studies use large samples to compare morbidity and mortality of married, divorced and single people
- Married men and women live longer and have fewer illnesses than single or divorced people
- Permanently single people have the highest mortality rate of any group
- Singleness has a poorer impact on men's life expectancy than women's
- Studies in the 1970s found that married men were happier than single men but married women were more likely to be depressed than single women

- Today, married people report higher levels of happiness and lower numbers of psychiatric symptoms than single or divorced people
- Single men and women have higher suicide rates at all ages than their married counterparts
- Today, marriage benefits appear to apply equally to men, women and gay couples
- Social isolation and loneliness are major risk factors for mental health problems

⊙ When relationships go badly: the effects of conflict on physiological functioning

Epidemiological studies provide a statistical measure of the link between relationship status and life expectancy whereas self-report measurements provide us with subjective accounts of well-being from different groups of people. However, these studies tell us little about the mechanisms by which these effects occur. In order to investigate these, research studies collecting material (bodily) data are used.

A growing body of research carried out over the past twenty or so years has demonstrated a range of physiological effects that arise from unhappy relationships and, specifically, from conflict between partners. In a review of the area, Kiecolt-Glaser and Newton (2001) examined the evidence from 64 studies that have looked at the relationship between marital interaction and different aspects of health. Dividing these by the different types of data obtained, Kiecolt-Glaser and Newton provide compelling evidence of the links between relationship conflict and a range of bodily systems including the cardiovascular system and the immune system.

The cardiovascular system

Many studies have demonstrated how stress from arguments can increase blood pressure and heart rate. Carels, Sherwood and Blumenthal (1998) found that women who were unhappily married showed greater increases in blood pressure and heart rates when asked to recall an argument with their partner, than those who were happily married.

Other studies have demonstrated that specific patterns of behaviour during conflicts seem to be most damaging to the cardiovascular system.

Ewart, Kraemer, Taylor and Agras (1991) studied a group of 24 women and 19 men who all had hypertension (high blood pressure) and asked them to carry out a 10-minute discussion with their partner about a relationship problem. Negative or hostile behaviour led to the greatest increase in blood pressure and heart rate in female participants: supportive or neutral behaviour had much less impact on the cardiovascular system. However, men showed increases in blood pressure only when the argument became fast and furious. Ewart et al. summarized their findings neatly by subtitling their report 'Not being nasty matters more than being nice'. It seems that hostility is not just bad for the relationship but is also bad for the body!

Stress hormones

Arguments also affect bodily systems that we are less aware of, as for example in the production of stress hormones such as **cortisol**. Kiecolt-Glaser and Newton (1993) examined the production of stress hormones when couples discussed a relationship problem. Blood samples were taken hourly from 8.00 in the morning until 10.00 at night from 90 newly married couples, aged on average 26 years old. These samples were pooled to provide a measurement of six key hormones related to stress. The couples were asked to discuss an area of conflict in their relationship in the morning to assess possible effects on stress hormones, which could be compared to the baseline levels.

The researchers found that women produced elevated levels of two particular stress hormones during the discussion, *cortisol and norepinephrine*. Production was highest if their husbands/partners responded to the conflict by withdrawal (you may recall the demand–withdrawal pattern we discussed in Chapter 5, Regulating relationships, which appears to be one of the most damaging forms of communication). In fact, arguments accounted for substantial variations of hormones (between 24% and 29%) across the day in women. In contrast, the men in Kiecolt-Glaser and Newton's study did not show fluctuating elevated hormones levels in response to arguments. In a second study, women's levels of cortisol elevated during an argument and remained high more than half an hour after the argument ended leaving the participants literally stewing in stress hormones (Fehm-Walfsdorf, Groth, Kaiser and Hahlweg, 1999). It seems that women are wired to respond to interpersonal conflict with increases in stress hormones.

Relationship conflict and the immune system

Other studies have examined how immune system functioning may be influenced by conflict and arguments, an area of research known as *psychoneuroimmunology*. Kiecolt-Glaser argues that the link between relationships and the functioning of the immune system is 'one of the most robust findings in psycho-neuroimmunology' (Kiecolt-Glaser, McGuire, Robles and Glaser, 2002: 539). It has long been thought that chronic stress leads to poorer immune functioning. For example, volunteers who had ongoing relationship difficulties are more likely to develop a cold when exposed to a virus in experimental conditions (Cohen et al., 1998).

However, as understanding of the complexity of the immune system develops, it is becoming apparent that chronic stress disrupts the working of the immune system but may actually increase some immune responses, such as the production of cytokines. Cytokines are substances that regulate inflammation. One type, anti-inflammatory cytokines, reduce inflammation whereas pro-inflammatory cytokines increase it. Increased production of cytokines is linked with premature ageing of the immune system. In 2003, Kiecolt-Glaser and colleagues examined the impact of chronic stress on a group of older, married people whose husband or wife had developed Alzheimer's disease. Over a period of about six years, Kiecolt-Glaser et al. found that the caring group had increased production of cytokines that was about four times the rate of the control group in a non-stressful marriage. The researchers concluded that chronic stress of this nature disrupted the immune system, effectively switching off the brakes that restrain inflammatory responses. This study is important as it suggests that stress has complex effects on immune functioning, disrupting different aspects.

These studies tell a simple story: relationships that involve negative interactions, stress or conflict bring a raft of temporary physical changes, which, over time, impact negatively on health (Kiecolt-Glaser and Newton, 2001). Some of these pathways are now reasonably well established. Relationship problems are also likely to have indirect effects on health. Stressed and unhappy people are more likely to engage in behaviours that put them at risk of health problems. They may be more likely to smoke and drink excessive amounts of alcohol, they tend to sleep less and to take less exercise. It is difficult to separate out the effects of these two kinds of factors. One challenge for health psychologists working within this area is to develop research methods that enable these factors to be separated.

⊙ When relationships go well: positive effects on health and happiness

So far, this chapter may have struck you as being rather gloomy. Conflict and arguments can mess you up mentally and physically! However, the other side to this is that good relationships provide all sorts of benefits: epidemiological studies indicate that they are linked with better emotional and physical health and longer life expectancy. There are other well-documented research studies that explore a wide range of benefits of personal relationships, both long and short term, which we will consider now.

Relationships affect our daily mood and emotions and most people report their highest levels of happiness and contentment when they are with friends or family. Larson (1990, cited in Miell and Dallos, 1996) asked a sample of students to take part in an unusual study, in which they were randomly paged at different times of the day and asked to record who they were with and their current state of happiness. Larson found that participants were most happy when they were with their friends, followed closely by family. People were least likely to feel happy when they were alone.

Relationships also influence self-esteem. Campbell, Sedikides and Bosson (1994) compared two groups of young students aged around 19. The first group (128) were engaged in a relationship whereas the second group (54) were currently unattached. The participants were asked to complete a range of measures including:

- A rating of their current self-esteem
- A measurement of the distance between their ideal and current selves
- A measurement of psychological well-being.

Campbell et al. found that the 'attached' group had less of a gap between their ideal and real self than those who were unattached. In addition, they reported significantly higher levels of psychological well-being. Of course, while these results show a relationship between self-esteem and relationship status, they cannot show cause and effect. It may be that people who feel better about themselves are more likely to enter into a relationship with a partner. However, these findings have been echoed by others working in the field.

What about effects of relationships on health? Many studies have shown that relationships link with better physical health: the more student roommates like each other, the fewer colds they get (Goleman, 1992) indicating a general level of health and resilience. Studies also indicate that happily married people are better at fending off infections (Kiecolt-Glaser et al., 1987). A longitudinal study using self-report measures was carried out by Prigerson, Maciejewski and Rosenheck (1999). The researchers found that happily married women reported better sleep and fewer visits to the doctor than those whose relationships were less happy. Hibbard and Pope (1993) selected a range of medical records randomly and compared life expectancy in different groups of women: those who lived the longest were happily married and reported high levels of equity and companionship in their relationships!

Many studies have pointed to the important role played by relationships in recovery from illness. In one study, women with advanced breast cancer who used a support group lived on average twice as long (37 months) as those who did not choose to attend a support group, demonstrating the powerful influence of social relationships. Similar findings were obtained in a study of heart attack survivors: the chances of surviving for more than a year were twice as high in elderly people who had social support (Berkman, Leo-Summers and Horowitz, 1992). Relationships may also help to maintain a healthy immune system: in one study, medical students who had good networks of friends showed a stronger immune response when given the Hepatitis B vaccine (Glaser et al., 1992).

Thinking scientifically →
The use of quasi-experimental research

It may have occurred to you as you read this section, that most of the studies reported here have involved the researchers making use of pre-existing groups of one kind or another. For example, studies using epidemiology have compared death rates in married, cohabiting, divorced and single individuals. The people in the samples belong to those categories and have not been allocated to them by the researcher as they would be in a true experiment. This may seem an obvious point – of course psychologists do not meddle in their participants' lives, to the extent of randomly allocating them to experimental conditions. This means that most of the studies in this area use a **quasi-experimental**, rather than truly experimental method.

Random allocation to conditions is an important principle in true experimental research as it enables the researcher to ensure that groups are comparable, rather than different from the start. When quasi-experimental methods are used, there is no way of knowing if the groups are equal to start with: it may be that people who experience relationship breakdown are different to those who stay together. One of the consequences of the use of quasi-experimental methods is the need to be cautious when drawing conclusions from research findings. It is much more difficult to say with conviction that X causes Y (for example divorce causes ill health). This may be because the two groups of people – those who stayed married and those who split up – may well be different from the start. This is sometimes referred to as the *selection hypothesis* as it takes the view that different groups of people select to stay in relationships, compared to those who choose to leave them.

Explaining the 'marriage benefit': How do good relationships enhance health?

Mastekaasa (1995) argues that the marriage benefit can be interpreted in a number of different ways:

- A secure relationship such as marriage may produce beneficial effects to the people involved. This is often known as the *protection hypothesis* as it takes the view that happy, secure relationships provide a range of factors that enhance health and protect against illness. Some of these factors could be practical. For example, increased financial resources arising from combined incomes of a dual-earning couple may provide opportunities for a higher standard of living and a healthier lifestyle in the form of diet, exercise and so on. Alternatively, secure relationships could lower stress levels and lead to less exposure to risks and illnesses, such as sexually transmitted infections. Perhaps the most important factor (and certainly one of the most frequently researched) is *social support*.
- Alternatively, it is possible that those who are happy and emotionally stable to start with are more likely to form lasting relationships – to get married and stay married. This approach is known as the *selection hypothesis*. It takes the opposite view to the protection hypothesis, as it assumes that emotional well-being causes two people to stay together.

- Finally, it is possible that a third underlying factor could cause lasting relationships and subjective well-being. This third factor could be something as simple as a stable personality.

The role of social support

The term social support is often used as a 'catch all' to describe the many different kinds of emotional activities that take place in intimate relationships. As we noted in Chapter 5, Regulating relationships, close relationships involve greater intimacy and opportunities for self-disclosure and sharing of feelings and fears, which reduces anxiety. Payne and Walker (1996) argue that social support may affect health in many different ways: partners could encourage each other to seek medical help if a potential problem (for example a suspicious lump) is found. They may also encourage greater compliance with medical treatment such as taking of medication. Alternatively, they may influence their partner towards a healthier lifestyle in terms of eating and exercise. Finally, the experience of being within a steady relationship might reduce contact with some potential hazards such as sexually transmitted infections.

Another important aspect of social support is the provision of practical help and information during crises. Reis and Franks (1994) examined the impact of both intimacy and social support on the health of a sample of 846 adults. Participants were selected from records at a medical centre and responded to a questionnaire asking them to comment on a variety of health and relationship indicators. The researchers found that the amount of social support given in the relationship predicted the health of partners. In most relationships, social support and intimacy were closely linked.

Social support does not simply happen face to face: increasingly, online communities such as groups on Facebook and other social networking sites may offer support in a virtual sense. Williams and Merten (2009) have examined the role played by sites such as Facebook in helping adolescents following the sudden death of a classmate. They examined the profiles/pages of 20 adolescents who had died between 2005 and 2007 and collected the comments posted by classmates and friends. They found that postings included comments or messages to the deceased along with memorial sentiments. Williams and Merten argue that postings of this nature help individuals to develop coping strategies as well as prolonging their attachment to the person who has died.

The effects of a support network

Other studies have demonstrated that the greater number of friends you have, the longer your life expectancy. Berkman and Syme (1979) studied 4725 married American adults aged between 30 and 69 years old. At Time 1 their health was assessed and they were asked about the social support they received from friends and family. This was divided into four categories:

- Support from marriage partner
- Support from close friends
- Support from family
- Support from social groups (church/sport and so on).

These figures were combined to give each person an overall 'Index of support' which related to how many connections they had. Nine years later the researchers followed them up with single question: who was still alive and who had died? They found strong relationships between the support index and life expectancy especially in women aged over 60. The higher the support index score and the number of connections, the more likely the person was still alive. The fewer connections, the greater the mortality rate (Table 8.2). Despite these compelling findings about friendship networks, we still do not know exactly how they work or the precise mechanisms which lead to these positive effects.

	Most connections		Least connections	
Age	Women	Men	Women	Men
30–49	1.5	2.4	6.9	6.4
50–59	7.3	9.6	15.3	30.8
60–69	9.7	21.8	29.4	39.4

Table 8.2 Social support index and mortality (Berkman and Syme, 1979)
Figures show the percentage of each age group who had died

Social support and gender differences

As you read this section, you may have noticed that there is something of a conundrum emerging here. Women appear to react more strongly in physiological terms to conflict in relationships. They show greater increases in blood pressure and stress hormones especially when arguments get nasty. These findings are particularly interesting as they reverse the normal pattern of stress responses which show that men usually have a greater physiological reactivity to stress (Kiecolt-Glaser and Newton, 2001). However, epidemiological studies have indicated that relationship breakdown/splitting up has a worse effect on men's health than women's, leading to higher morbidity and mortality. In addition, single men have a much higher rate of early death than single women. How can these differences be explained?

One argument put forward by Kiecolt-Glaser and Newton (2001) is centred on social support. Women tend to have larger social support networks than men: they are more likely to use a range of close friends for social support during crises on a one to one basis. In contrast, men have smaller support networks. Their networks of male friends are often group-oriented (for example work or sports groups) and many men rely on their partner for emotional support. When this relationship gets into difficulties or breaks down, this may deprive a man of his main confidant and source of social support, while women's support networks are less disrupted by break-ups. Another explanation is that women often attempt to take control over other people's health and may propel their partner to the doctor when problems arise!

What about pets?

Before we leave the topic of effects, this chapter (and indeed entire book) has focused exclusively on human relationships. But while you have been reading this chapter, you may have thought in passing about 'cross-species' relationships or those that we have with our pets. Anyone who has known the friendship and comfort of a friendly dog or cat will know that a great deal of social support can be offered from such relationships. A whole range of studies have drawn attention to the role of pets in health and happiness and within specific therapeutic settings. Some of these benefits include lower rates of depression (Siegal, 1990), the reduction of stress levels, and providing comfort following bereavement (Adkins and Rajecki, 1999). Physically, pet owners have lower rates of heart disease and cholesterol (Allen, 2001). Anderson, Reid and Jennings (1992) found that non-pet owners had higher blood pressure and levels of plasma triglycerides than pet owners. The most common explanation for this is the benefit of increased exercise through regular dog walking. Wood, Gilesw-Corti, Bulsara and Bosch (2007) carried out a study in Australia, collecting quantitative data via survey and qualitative data through discussion/focus groups. They found that dog owners referred almost universally to the social benefits of having dogs: these included chatting to new people on walks. Pets were seen as 'an antidote to loneliness' leading to social contact and interactions.

A study by Headey, Na and Zheng (2008) in China has compared the physical health and well-being of dog owners and non-dog owners using objective and self-report measures. Dog ownership in towns and cities was banned in China until 1992, but has grown rapidly since then. Dog owners were found to take more frequent exercise, to sleep better (perhaps related to exercise) and to have better self-report of health and fitness. In terms of objective measures, they made fewer visits to doctors and took fewer days off work than non-dog owners.

◉ Chapter summary

- Physiological studies demonstrate that relationships have a range of immediate effects on health
- Conflict leads to increases in blood pressure especially for those with hypertension. Negative and hostile behaviour seems to be most damaging to the cardiovascular system
- Women produce elevated levels of stress hormones, including cortisol and norepinephrine, during arguments
- The immune system is also effected by conflict
- Happy relationships are associated with better mental and physical health
- Happily married women are better at fighting off colds and other infections: they also report better sleep and make fewer visits to the doctor
- Social support also influences survival and recovery after serious illnesses such as heart attacks
- Gender differences may be partially explained by social support
- Many studies use quasi-experimental designs, as participants fall into pre-existing groups and are not randomly allocated to conditions. This makes it difficult to establish if there are differences between groups
- Relationships with pets provide emotional benefits and social support

⊙ Further reading

A good coverage of research on social support is given in Banyard, P. (1995) *Applying Psychology to Health,* Hodder and Stoughton.

Duck, S. (ed.) with Silver, R.C. (1990) *Personal relationships and Social Support* contains a series of chapters looking at support provided in personal relationships.

Useful introductory texts on health psychology:

Ogden, J. (2007) *Health Psychology,* McGraw Hill/Open University Press.

Morrison, V. and Bennett, P. (2006) *An Introduction to Health Psychology,* Pearson.

Glossary

Acculturative stress The stress experienced from living in a culture where views, values and practices clash with the beliefs of one's own culture

Acculturation The process of internalizing the views of a different culture, for example the desire for voluntary, non-arranged marriages in some second and third generation British Asians

Adult attachment interview A method devised by Main to classify adults into different attachment styles. The narrative is analysed for *how* the individual talks about their past and present relationships, as well as what they say

Anxiety One dimension of Brennan, Clark and Shaver's attachment model. People vary in their degree of anxiety in relationships with some being highly anxious and others being much less worried

Arranged marriages One of the most common forms of marriage arrangement across the globe in collectivist cultures and in many religious groups. Parents or well-wishers select potential partners for their offspring based on criteria including education and background. There are considerable variations in how much choice young people have to accept or reject partners

Attachment A relationship between two people that involves closeness, distress on separation and joy on reunion

Attachment type A characteristic way of behaving in childhood and adult relationships, generally divided into secure or insecure. Attachment type can be assessed by the strange situation in infants and by the adult attachment interview in adults

Avoidance Second dimension of Brennan, Clark and Shaver's attachment model referring to fear of involvement or being hurt in relationships

Barriers to dissolution Factors in long-term relationships that make it more difficult for a couple to split up, such as shared property, joint friends or children

Behaviourism A perspective which assumes that much human behaviour is the result of learning, through classical and operant conditioning

Big Five Personality Inventory Widely used method of measuring personality devised by Costa and McCrae using five dimensions: openness, conscientiousness, extroversion, agreeableness and neuroticism (OCEAN)

Bogus stranger technique A method used by Byrne in which he created a profile of another unreal (bogus) person to assess the importance of attitude similarity

Bride price A sum of money paid by the groom's family to the father of a bride for her value, before a marriage takes place. A common practice in traditional hunter-gatherer societies

Collectivist culture One of Hofstede's four cultural dimensions. Collectivist cultures value the input from family and social groups in decision making and in shaping personal identity. Asian nations such as Pakistan are strongly collectivist

Commitment An important aspect of serious relationships, expressed by a desire to stay together even when things get tough

Communal relationships Concept proposed by Clark and Mills to describe relationships in which rewards are given to meet a partner's needs without an expectation that they will be paid back

Comparison level Concept of social exchange theory suggesting that we compare current relationships to those we have had in the past to see if they are better or worse

Comparison level for alternatives Concept of social exchange theory suggesting that we compare our current relationship with potential relationships we could have with other people to see if it is worth continuing

Content analysis A method of analysing spoken/written data by counting the number of times something occurs

Continuity hypothesis A core concept of Bowlby's attachment theory which suggests that early attachment style continues and influences later relationships

Cortisol A stress hormone which increases during conflict and arguments

Critical social psychology A recent form of social psychology which challenges the experimental social perspective and advocates the use of qualitative research methods

Culture A group of people who share history, beliefs and values, for example a racial, regional or religious group

Culture blind A theory that has not been tested outside the culture in which it was developed

Culture bound Research that has been carried out using a sample made up of people from the same cultural background

Developmental social psychology A perspective that considers how social development takes place across the lifespan. Developmental social psychologists are interested in the role of attachments

Discourse analysis A qualitative method of analysing talk and conversation

Discursive social psychology An influential perspective in critical social psychology which advocates the use of qualitative methods such as discourse analysis

Dunbar's number An evolutionary concept, which suggests that we can have stable social relationships with around 150 people. This number is thought to be related to the size of the neocortex

Earned security A concept proposed by Main, Kaplan and Cassidy to describe people who have had early problematic attachments/relationships in childhood but have become secure later in life through positive adult relationships

Economic theories A group of theories of relationship maintenance which suggest that people run relationships in a similar way to bank accounts, keeping an eye on what they and their partner put in and get out

Environment of Evolutionary Adaptation Period of time between 40,000 and 10,000 years ago when early humans lived in small groups and followed a hunter-gatherer lifestyle. Many of today's human behaviours are thought to have evolved during this period of time

Epidemiology The study of how many illnesses occur in different groups such as married, divorced and single people

Equity theory An economic theory of relationship maintenance which suggests that partners want rewards to be proportional to what they input to the relationship

Ethology The observation and description of animal behaviours in the natural environment

Evolutionary social psychology A recent perspective, which is based on Darwin's theory of evolution and sociobiology. Evolutionary social psychology argues that many of today's behaviours and tendencies have their roots in our ancestral past

Exchange relationships Concept proposed by Clark and Mills to describe relationships in which rewards are given with the expectation that similar rewards will be paid back

Experiences in Close Relationships Scale A 36-item scale measuring feelings of anxiety and avoidance in close relationships

Experimental social psychology An influential perspective in modern social psychology which uses quantitative methods and focuses on how people think and interpret their social worlds

Factor analysis A statistical technique used to look for patterns in large amounts of data

Field of availables Concept proposed by Kerckhoff and Davis's filter theory to refer to the total group from which partners could theoretically be chosen

Field of desirables Concept proposed by Kerckhoff and Davis's filter theory to refer to people who we would define as desirable, suitable partners in terms of age, social background, education and so on

Filter theory A theory of relationship formation which argues that different factors are important at different times, so unsuitable partners are filtered out

Health psychology A branch of psychology which considers how health and illness are influenced by psychological factors

Horizontal relationship A relationship between two people of similar age, status and power such as siblings or peers

Individualistic cultures Cultures which value independence, competition and achievement. The UK and USA are strongly individualistic

Insecure-ambivalent attachment An attachment type identified by Ainsworth in the strange situation, characterized by lack of trust in childhood, fear of abandonment in adulthood along with a tendency to be jealous

Insecure-avoidant attachment An attachment type identified by Ainsworth in the strange situation, characterized by avoidance of relationships in childhood and fear of involvement or commitment in adulthood

Interdependence theory An explanation of relationship maintenance which suggests that couples stay together due to investments and feelings of commitment

Interpersonal attraction A positive evaluation of another person along with the desire to get to know them more

Inter-sexual selection A component of Darwin's theory of sexual selection. Inter-sexual selection occurs when members of one sex (often females) choose mates from the other sex on the basis of their attributes

Internal working model An aspect of Bowlby's attachment theory which suggests that children form a model of themselves, of other people and of relationships in general from their first attachment

Interpretative repertoires A concept in discursive social psychology. Repertoires are cultural ideas used to make sense of and explain the world

Intra-sexual selection A component of Darwin's theory of sexual selection. Intra-sexual selection takes place when members of one sex (often males) compete for access to the other sex (usually females) in various ways including fighting

Investments Things that have been put into a relationship, such as time, that cannot be got back out if the relationship ends

Law of attraction Concept proposed by Byrne suggesting that we like people who share similar attitudes, values and beliefs to ourselves

Life expectancy The average age at which men and women die

Longitudinal research Research studies in which the same group of participants are followed up several times

Maintenance The processes involved in keeping a relationship going including communication, negotiation and dealing with conflict

Matching hypothesis Concept proposed by Murstein suggesting that relationships are formed between people with similar levels of physical attractiveness

Mate preference Factors that are sought in potential partners, such as physical attractiveness, a sense of humour, youth and high income

Material data Data obtained using physiological measurements such as heart rate and blood pressure

Meta-theory A theoretical approach which includes a smaller number of theories, sharing similar principles. Economic theory of relationship maintenance is a meta-theory encompassing exchange, equity and investment theories

Minimax principle A concept in social exchange theory which argues that people wish to minimize the costs in their relationships while maximizing the rewards

Morbidity rate A measurement of how many illnesses people develop

Mortality rate A measurement of how many people die in a specific social group

Natural selection A concept proposed by Charles Darwin. Natural selection is the process by which behaviours or bodily features that increase the chance of survival are passed on to offspring

Outcome A concept in economic theories suggesting that any relationship at any time can be judged to be in state of profit or loss depending on the relative rewards and costs

Parental investment theory An evolutionary theory proposed by Trivers (1972) which suggests that women invest more than men in offspring and are consequently choosy in who they will mate with. Men invest less in offspring and are therefore less choosy

Parental investment Term used in evolutionary theories to refer to the amount of input from males and females to their offspring. Investment is made up of mating effort and rearing effort

Perspectives Ways of studying a topic that make assumptions about what should be studied and the methods that should be used. Perspectives are sometimes known as approaches

Predisposing factors Factors within one partner which make a relationship more likely to break down, such as drug or alcohol abuse

Qualitative methods Research methods that involve collecting and analysing data which is non-numeric, often written or verbal data

Quantitative methods Research methods that involve collecting and analysing numeric data

Quasi-experimental method Partially experimental or having some features of an experiment. Comparisons between males and females are quasi-experimental as they cannot be randomly allocated to conditions

Random allocation Putting participants in experimental conditions using a random method. An important principle of experimental design

Reproductive success Concept from the evolutionary perspective which refers to the number of surviving offspring left by an individual

Reward/need satisfaction theory Relationships are formed with people who provide rewards and meet our needs

Rewards Factors exchanged in relationships which are enjoyable

Safe base According to Bowlby's attachment theory, securely attached children use their mother as a safe base who can be returned to when the environment becomes stressful

Secure attachment An attachment type identified by Ainsworth in the strange situation, characterized in childhood by distress on separation and joy at reunion. Securely attached adults are generally trusting of partners and are not afraid of being abandoned or hurt

Sexual dimorphism Concept in the evolutionary perspective, referring to bodily differences between male and female members of a species. In humans, males tend to be larger than females (and hairier!)

Sexual selection Concept proposed by Charles Darwin suggesting that bodily features that enhance attractiveness to the opposite sex, such as the peacock's tail, are likely to be passed on to offspring

Sexual strategies theory A type of evolutionary theory proposed by Buss and Schmidt suggesting that human sexual behaviour involves long- and short-term relationships with different kinds of qualities sought in partners

Social desirability Tendency of participants to provide socially acceptable answers to interview questions

Social exchange theory An economic theory proposed by Homans suggesting that people aim to maximize their rewards and minimize costs in their relationships

Social learning theory A theory within the behavioural perspective which suggests that many behaviours, such as the ability to make friends, are learned through observation of role models and copying of their behaviour

Strange situation A laboratory-based method devised by Mary Ainsworth for observing, measuring and classifying attachment types in small infants

Triangulation The use of multiple research methods to collect data and provide a rounded picture of an issue

Two factor model A model proposed by Gottman which predicts when couples will split up depending on their type of communication and way of dealing with conflict

References

Adkins, S. and Rajecki, D. (1999) Pets' roles in parents' bereavement. *Anthrozoös*, 12, 33–42.

Afifi, W.S., Falato, W.L. and Weiner, J.L. (2001) Identity concerns following a severe relational transgression: The role of discovery method for the relational outcomes of infidelity. *Journal of Social and Personal Relationships*, 18(2): 291–308.

Afifi, T.O., Cox, B.J. and Enns, M. (2006) Mental health profiles among married, never married and separated/divorced mothers in a national representative sample. *Social Psychiatry Psychiatric Epidemiology*, 41: 122–9.

Ainsworth, M.D.S., Bell, S.M.V. and Staydon, D.J. (1971) Individual differences in strange situation behaviour of one year olds. In Durkin, K. (1998) *Developmental Social Psychology*. Oxford: Blackwell.

Alexy, A.M. (2008) Intimate separations: Divorce and its reverberations in contemporary Japan, *Dissertation Abstracts International Section a: Humanities and Social Sciences*, 69(6-A): 2329.

Allen, K. (2001) *Dog ownership and control of borderline hypertension: A controlled randomized trial*. 22nd Annual Scientific Sessions of the Society of Behavioral Medicine. Seattle, Washington.

Allport, G.W. (1935) Attitudes. In Hogg, M.A and Vaughan, G.M. (4th edn) (2005) *Social Psychology*, Harlow: Pearson Prentice Hall.

Al-Thakeb, F.T. (1985) The Arab family and modernity: Evidence from Kuwait. In Goodwin, R. (1999) *Personal Relationships Across Cultures*, London: Routledge.

Amato, P.R. (1999) Children of divorced parents as young adults. In Hetherington, M.E. (ed.) *Coping with Divorce, Single Parenting and*

Marriage: A Risk and Resiliency Perspective, Mahwah, NJ: Lawrence Erlbaum.

Amato, P.R. and Rogers, S.J. (1997) A longitudinal study of marital problems and subsequent divorce. *Journal of Marriage and the Family*, 59(3): 612–24.

Anderson, J.L, Crawford, C.B., Nadeau, J. and Lindberg, T. (1992) Was the Duchess of Windsor right? A cross-cultural study of the socio ecology of ideals of female body shape. In Barrett, L., Dunbar, R. and Lycett, J. (2002) *Human Evolutionary Psychology*, Basingstoke: Palgrave Macmillan.

Anderson, W., Reid, C. and Jennings, G. (1992) Pet ownership and risk factors for cardiovascular disease. *Medical Journal of Australia*, 157: 298–301.

Angier, N. (1990) Anger can ruin more than your day. In Smith, E. and Mackie, D. (2000) Social *Psychology*, Hove: Psychology Press.

Argyle, M. (1987) The psychology of happiness. In Gross, R.D. (1993) (3rd edn) *Psychology: The Science of Mind and Behaviour*, Bath: Hodder and Stoughton.

Argyle, M. (1996) The experimental study of relationships. In Miell, D. and Dallos, R. (1996) *Social Interaction and Personal Relationships*, Milton Keynes: Open University Press.

Argyle, M. and Henderson, M. (1985) The rules of relationships. In Goodwin, R. (1999) *Personal Relationships Across Cultures*, London: Routledge.

Astana, A. and Campbell, D. (2009) Divorce rates linked to age and schooling, *The Observer* 27.09.2009.

Bailey, J. and Zucker, K. (1995) Childhood sex-typed behavior and sexual orientation: A conceptual analysis and quantitative review. *Developmental Psychology*, 31(1). Special issue: Sexual orientation and human development, pp. 43–55.

Banyard, P. (1995) *Applying Psychology to Health*, Hodder and Stoughton.

Barber, N. (1995) The evolutionary psychology of physical attractiveness: sexual selection and human morphology. In Barrett, L., Dunbar, R. and Lycett, J. (2002) *Human Evolutionary Psychology*, Basingstoke: Palgrave Macmillan.

Barrett, L., Dunbar, R. and Lycett, J. (2002) *Human Evolutionary Psychology*, Basingstoke: Palgrave Macmillan.

Batabyal, A. (2001) On the likelihood of finding the right partner in an arranged marriage. *The Journal of Socio-Economics*, 30(3): 2273–80.

Baxter, L. (1986) Gender differences in the heterosexual relationship rules embedded in break-up accounts, *Journal of Social and Personal Relationships*, 3(3): 289–306.

Beach, S.R., Fincham, F.D. and Katz, J. (1998) Marital therapy in the treatment of depression: Toward a third generation of therapy and research. In Kiecolt-Glaser, J.K. and Newton, T.L. (2001) *Marriage and Health: His and Hers. Psychological Bulletin*, 127(4): 472–503.

Becker, C.S. (1988) Unbroken ties: Lesbian ex-lovers. In Dwyer, D. (2000) *Interpersonal Relationships*, London: Routledge.

Bee, H. (1995) *The Developing Child*, New York: Harper-Collins.

Berkman, L.F., Leo-Summers, C. and Horowitz, R.I. (1992) Emotional support and survival after myocardial infarction: A prospective population based study of the elderly. In Smith, E. and Mackie, D. (2000) *Social Psychology*, Hove: Psychology Press.

Berkman, L. and Syme, S.L. (1979) Social networks, host resistance and mortality. In Miell, D. and Dallos, R. (1996) *Social Interaction and Personal Relationships*, Milton Keynes: Open University Press.

Berry, J.W. (1984) Multicultural policy in Canada: A social psychological analysis. In Hogg, M.A. and Vaughan, G.M. (4th edn) (2005) *Social Psychology*, Harlow: Pearson Prentice Hall.

Betzig, L. (1989) Causes of conjugal dissolution: A cross-cultural study. In Goodwin, R. (1999) *Personal Relationships Across Cultures*, London: Routledge.

Birnbaum, M.G. (2009) Taking Goffman on a tour of Facebook: College students and the presentation of self in a mediated digital environment. *Dissertation abstracts International Section A: Humanities and Social Sciences*, 69(8-A): 3055.

Black, K. and Schutte, E. (2006) Recollections of being loved: Implications of childhood experiences with parents for young adults' romantic relationships. *Journal of Family Issues*, 27: 1459–80.

Blanchard, R. and Bogaert, A. (1996) Biodemographic comparisons of homosexual and heterosexual men in the Kinsey interview data. *Archives of Sexual Behavior*, 25(6): 551–79.

Borgerhoff Mulder, M. (1988) Kipsigis bride wealth payments. In Barrett, L., Dunbar, R. and Lycett, J. (2002) *Human Evolutionary Psychology*, Basingstoke: Palgrave Macmillan.

Bossard, J. (1932) 'Residential propinquity as a factor in marriage selection' cited in Eysenck, M. (2001) *Psychology for A2 Level*, Hove: Psychology Press.

Bowlby, J. (1969) *Attachment and Loss. Vol. 1: Attachment*, New York: Basic Books.

Brehmn, S.S. (1992) *Intimate Relationships*, New York: McGraw Hill.

Brennan, K., Clark, C. and Shaver, P. (1998) Self report measurement of adult attachment; An integrative overview. In Simpson, J. and Rholes, W.S. (eds) (1998) *Attachment Theory and Close Relationships*, New York, NY: Guilford Press.

Bruce, V. and Young, A. (1998) *In the Eye of the Beholder: The Science of Face Perception*. New York: Oxford University Press.

Buss, D.M. (1989) Sex differences in human mate preferences: Evolutionary hypotheses tested in 37 cultures. *Behavioural and Brain Sciences*, 12: 1–49 Cited in *Challenging Psychological Issues*, Milton Keynes: Open University Press.

Buss, D.M. (1990) International preferences in selecting mates: A study of 37 cultures. *Journal of Cross Cultural Psychology*, 21: 5–47.

Buss, D M., Larsen, R.J., Westen, D. and Semmelroth, J. (1992) Sex differences in jealousy: Evolution, physiology, and psychology. *Psychological Science*, 3(4): 251–5.

Buss, D. and Schmidt, D.P. (1993) Sexual strategies theory: An evolutionary perspective on human mating. *Psychological Review*, 100: 204–32.

Byrne, D. (1971) *The Attraction Paradigm*, New York: Academic Press.

Campbell, W.K., Sedikides, C. and Bosson, J. (1994) Romantic Involvement, self-discrepancy and psychological well being: A preliminary investigation. *Personal Relationships*, 1(4): 399–404.

Carels, R.A., Sherwood, A. and Blumenthal, J.A. (1998) Psychosocial influences on blood pressure during daily life. In Kiecolt-Glaser, J.K. and Newton, T.L. (2001) Marriage and Health: His and Hers. *Psychological Bulletin*, 127(4): 472–503.

Cassidy, J. and Berlin, L.J. (1994) The insecure ambivalent pattern of attachment: Theory and research. *Child Development*, 65: 971–91.

Clark, M. and Mills, J. (1979) Interpersonal attraction in exchange and communal relationships. *Journal of Personality and Social Psychology*, 37(1): 12–24.

Clark, R.D. and Hatfield, E. (1989) Gender differences in receptivity to sexual offers. *Journal of Psychology and Human Sexuality*, 2: 39–55.

Clegg, H. (2007) Evolutionary Psychology. In Miell, D., Phoenix, A. and Thomas, K. (2007) *Mapping Psychology Book 1*, Milton Keynes: Open University Press.

Cohen, S., Frank, E., Doyle, W.J., Skoner, D.P., Rabin, B.S. and Gwaltney, J.M. (1998) Types of stressors that increase susceptibility to the common cold in healthy adults. In Kiecolt-Glaser, J.K. and Newton, T.L. (2001) Marriage and Health: His and Hers. *Psychological Bulletin*, 127(4): 472–503.

Cooper, T. and Roth, I. (2007) *Challenging Psychological Issues*. Milton Keynes: Open University Press.

Coyle, A. (1993) A study of psychological well-being among gay men using the GHQ-30. *British Journal of Clinical Psychology*, 32(2): 218–20.

Cunningham, M.R. (1986) Measuring the physical in physical attractiveness: Quasi experiments on the socio-biology of female facial beauty. *Journal of Personality and Social Psychology*, 50(5): 925–35.

Cunningham, M.R., Barbee, A.P. and Pike, C.L. (1990) What do women want?: Facialmetric assessment of multiple motives in the perception of male facial attractiveness. *Journal of Personality and Social Psychology*, 59: 61–72.

Cupach, W.R. and Metts, S. (1995) The role of sexual attitude similarity in romantic heterosexual relationships. *Personal Relationships*, 2(4): 287–300.

d'Ardenne, P. and Mahtani, A. (1990) *Transcultural Counselling in Action*, London: Sage.

Darwin, C. (1859) *The Origin of the Species*, London: Murray.

Darwin, C. (1871) The descent of man and selection in relation to sex. In Barrett, L., Dunbar, R. and Lycett, J. (2002) *Human Evolutionary Psychology*, Basingstoke: Palgrave Macmillan.

de Maris, A. (2007) The role of relationship inequity in marital disruption. *Journal of Social and Personal Relationships*, 24(2): 177–95.

De Munck, V. (1998) Lust, love and arranged marriages in Sri Lanka. In de Munck, V. *Romantic Love and Sexual Behaviour: Perspectives from the Social Sciences*, Westport: Greenwood Publishing Group.

Deaux, K., Dane, F.C. and Wrightsman, L.S. (1993) *Social Psychology in the 90's*, California: Brooks Cole.

Deaux, K.K. and Hanna, R. (1984) Courtship in the personal column. In Smith, E.R. and Mackie, D. (2000) *Social Psychology*, Hove: Psychology Press.

Detter, J. (2006) Attention to romantic alternative; Internet daters and traditional daters compared. *Dissertation Abstracts International: Section B*, 67: 1145.

Dwyer, D. (2000) *Interpersonal Relationships*, London: Routledge.

Duck, S.W. (1984) *Personal Relationships 4*, London and New York: Academic Press.

Duck, S.W. (1986) *Human Relationships: An Introduction to Social Psychology*, Thousand Oaks, CA: Sage.

Duck, S.W. (1992) *Human Relationships* (2nd edn), London: Sage.

Duck, S.W. (1994) *Meaningful Relationships: Talking, Sense and Relating*, Thousand Oaks, CA: Sage.

Dunbar, R. and Waynforth, D. (1995) Lonely hearts analysis. Cited in R. Dunbar (1995) Are you lonesome tonight? *New Scientist*, 145(1964), 26–31.

Dunne, G. (1997) *Lesbian Lifestyles: Women's Work and the Politics of Sexuality*, London: Macmillan – now Palgrave Macmillan.

Durkin, K. (1995) *Developmental Social Psychology*. Oxford: Blackwell.

Ekman, P. and Friesen, W.V. (1978) Facial action coding system. In Gottman, J.M. and Levenson, R.W (1992) Marital processes predictive of later dissolution: Behaviour, physiology and health. *Journal of Personality and Social Psychology*, 63: 221–3.

Ewart, C.K., Taylor, C.B., Kraemer, H.C. and Agras, W.S. (1991) High blood pressure and marital discord: Not being nasty matters more than being nice. *Health Psychology*, 10(3): 155–63.

Feeney, J.A. and Noller, P. (1991) Attachment style and verbal descriptions of romantic partners. In Shulman, S., Scharf, M., Lumer, D. and Maurer, O. (2001) Parental divorce and young adult children's romantic relationships: Resolution of the divorce experience. *American Journal of Orthopsychiatry*, 71(4): 473–8.

Feeney, J.A. and Noller, P. (1992) Attachment style and romantic love: Relationship dissolution. *Australian Journal of Psychology*, 44(2): 69–74.

Fehm-Wolfsdorf, G., Groth, T., Kaiser, A. and Hahlweg, K. (1999) Cortisol responses to marital conflict depend on marital interaction quality. *International Journal of Behavioural Medicine*, 6(3): 207–27.

Festinger, L., Schachter, S., and Back, K. (1950) Social pressures in informal groups: A study of human factors in housing. In Smith, E. and Mackie, D. (2000) *Social Psychology*. Hove: Psychology Press.

Fiske, S.T. (1998) Stereotyping, prejudice and discrimination. In Hogg, M.A. and Vaughan, G.M. (4th edn) (2005) *Social Psychology*, Harlow: Pearson Prentice Hall.

Fiske, A.P., Kitayama, S., Marcus, H.R., and Nesbitt, R.E (1998) The cultural matrix of social psychology. In Hogg and Vaughan (2005).

Fitzgerald, S.B. (2004) Making the transition: Understanding the longevity of lesbian relationships. In *Lesbian Ex-lovers: The Really Long-term Relationships*. Weinstock, Jacqueline S. and Rothblum, Esther D. (eds); pp. 177–92. Binghamton, NY, US: Harrington Park Press/The Haworth Press.

Forssell, S.L. (2005) Gay male couples: Extra dyadic sexual activity, psychological adjustment, relationship quality and HIV risk. *Dissertation Abstracts International: Section B: The Sciences and Engineering*, 65(7-B): 3772.

Frederick, D., Salska, I., Pawlowski, B., Reilly, A., Laird, K. and Rudd, N. (2008) Conditional mate preferences: Factors influencing preferences for height. *Personality and Individual Differences*, 44(1): 203–15.

Ghuman, P.A.S (1994) Canadian or Indo Canadian?: A study of South Asian adolescents. In Goodwin, R. (1999) *Personal Relationships Across Cultures*, London: Routledge.

Glaser, R., Kiecolt-Glaser, J.K., Bonneau, R.H., Malarkey, W., Kennedy, S. and Hughes, J. (1992) Stress induced modulation of the immune response to recombinant hepatitis B vaccine. *Psychosomatic Medicine*, 54: 22–9.

Goffman, E. (1956) *The Presentation of Self in Everyday Life*, Edinburgh: Edinburgh University Press.

Goleman, D. (1990) Support groups may do more in cancer than relieve the mind. In Smith, E. and Mackie, D. (2000) *Social Psychology*, Hove: Psychology Press.

Goleman, D. (1992) New light on how stress erodes health. *The New York Times*, 15 December 1992.

Goleman, D. (2006) *Social Intelligence: The new science of human relationships*. New York: Bantam Books.

Goodwin, R. (1999) *Personal Relationships Across Cultures*, London: Routledge.

Goodwin, R. (2005) Why I study relationships and culture. *The Psychologist*, 18(10).

Goodwin, R. and Pillay, U. (2006) Relationships, culture and Social Change. In Vangelista, N. and Perlman, D. (eds) *The Cambridge Handbook of Personal Relationships*, New York: Cambridge University Press.

Goodwin, R. and Tang, D. (1991) Preferences for friends and close relationship partners: Cross cultural comparisons. *Journal of Social Psychology*, 131: 579–81.

Goodwin, R., Adatia, K., Sinhal, H., Cramer, D. and Ellis, P. (1997) Social support and marital well being in an Asian community. In Goodwin, R. (1999) *Personal Relationships Across Cultures.* London: Routledge.

Gottman, J. (2002) A two factor model for predicting when a couple will divorce: Exploratory analyses using 14 year longitudinal data. *Family Processes,* 41(1): 83–96.

Gottman, J.M. and Levenson, R.W (1992) Marital processes predictive of later dissolution: Behaviour, physiology and health. *Journal of Personality and Social Psychology*, 63: 221–3.

Gottman, J.M., Levenson, R.W., Gross, J., Frederickson, B., McCoy, K., Rosenthal, L., Ruef, A. and Yosimoto, D. (2003) Correlates of gay and lesbian couples relationship satisfaction and relationship dissolution. *Journal of Homosexuality,* 45(1): 23–43.

Gough, B. and McFadden, M. (2001) *Critical social Psychology.* Basingstoke: Palgrave Macmillan.

Gove, W. (1972) The relationship between sex roles, marital status and mental illness. *Social Forces,* 51.

Gove, W. and Tudor, J. (1973) Adult sex roles and mental illness. *American Journal of Sociology*, 77: 812–35.

Gray, J. (1992) *Men are from Mars, Women are from Venus*, New York: HarperCollins.

Gruber-Baldini, A.L., Schaie, K.W. and Willis, S.L. (1995) Similarity in married couples: a longitudinal study of mental abilities and rigidity-flexibility. In Barrett, L., Dunbar, R. and Lycett, J. (2002) *Human Evolutionary Psychology*, Basingstoke: Palgrave Macmillan.

Gupta, U. and Singh, P. (1982) An exploratory study of love and liking and type of marriages. *Indian Journal of Applied Psychology*, 19(2): 92–7.

Guerrero, L. and Chavez, A. (2005) Relational maintenance in cross sex friendships characterised by different types of romantic intent: An exploratory study. *Western Journal of Communication*, 69(4): 339–58.

Guerrero, L.K. and Mongeau, P.A. (2008) On becoming 'more than friends': The transition from friendship to romantic relationship. In Sprecher, S., Wenzel, A. and Harvey, J. (eds) *Handbook of Relationships Initiation*, New York, NY: Psychology Press.

Guru, S. (2009) Divorce: Obstacles and opportunities: South Asian women in Britain. *The Sociological Review*, 57(2): 285–305.

Gutierrez-Lobos, K., Wolfl, G., Scherer, M., Anderer, P. and Schmidl-Mohl, B. (2000) The generation gap in depression reasons: The influence of marital and employment status on the female/male ratio of treated incidence rates. *Social Psychiatry. Psychiatric Epidemiology*, 35: 202–10.

Hahlweg, K., Markman, H.J., Thurmaier, F., Engl, J. and Eckert, V. (1998) Prevention of marital distress: results of a German prospective longitudinal study. *Journal of Family Psychology*, 12(4): 543–56.

Hall, K.A. (2000) Gender, marital status and psychiatric disorder: An examination of social causation versus social selection explanations for the gender specific benefits of marriage on mental health. *Dissertation Abstracts International: Humanities and Social Sciences*, 60(10-A).

Hamilton, C.E. (1994) Continuity and discontinuity of attachment from infancy through adolescence. In Cooper, T. and Roth, I. (2007) *Challenging Psychological Issues*, Milton Keynes: Open University Press.

Harlow, H.F. and Harlow, M.K. (1962) Social deprivation in monkeys. *Scientific American*, 207: 136–46.

Harris, J.R. (1995) Where is the child's environment? A group socialization theory of development. *Psychological Review*, 102: 458–89.

Hartup, W.W. (1989) Social relationships and their developmental significance. In Durkin, K. (1995) *Developmental Social Psychology*, Oxford: Blackwell.

Hatfield, E. and Sprecher, S. (1995) Men's and women's mate preferences in the United States, Russia and Japan. In Goodwin, R. (1999) *Personal Relationships Across Cultures*, London: Routledge.

Hatfield, E., Traupmann-Pillemer, J. and O'Brien, M.U. (1990) Global and detailed measures of equity/inequity. In Van Yperen, N. and Buunk, B. A longitudinal study of equity and satisfaction in intimate relationships. *European Journal of Social Psychology*, 20: 287–309.

Hazan, C. and Shaver, P. (1987) Romantic love conceptualized as an attachment process. *Journal of Personality and Social Psychology*, 52(3): 511–24.

Heady, B., Na, F. and Zheng, R. (2008) Pet dogs benefit owners' health: A natural experiment in China. *Social Indicators Research,* 87(3): 481–93.

Hendrick, S.S. (1988). A generic measure of relationship satisfaction. *Journal of Marriage and the Family, 50,* 93–8.

Hibbard, J.H. and Pope, C.R. (1993) The quality of social roles as predictors of morbidity and mortality. In Kiecolt-Glaser, J.K. and Newton, T.L. (2001) *Marriage and Health: His and Hers. Psychological Bulletin,* 127(4): 472–503.

Hickson, F.C., Davies, P.M. Hunt, A.J. and Weatherburn, P. (1992) Maintenance of open gay relationships: Some strategies for protection against HIV. *AIDS Care,* 4(4): 409–19.

Hill, C.T., Rubin, Z. and Peplau, L.A. (1976) Breakups before marriage: The end of 103 affairs. *Journal of Social Issues,* 32(1): 147–68.

Hillier, L. and Mitchell, A. (2008) It was as useful as a chocolate kettle: Sex education in the lives of same sex attracted young people in Australia. *Sex Education,* 8(2): 211–24.

Hoem, B. and Hoem, J.M. (1988) The Swedish family: Aspects of contemporary developments. In Goodwin, R. (1999) *Personal Relationships Across Cultures,* London: Routledge.

Hofstede, G. (1980) Cultures consequences: International differences in work related values. In Hogg, M.A. and Vaughan, G.M. (4th edn) (2005) *Social Psychology,* Harlow: Pearson Prentice Hall.

Hogg, M.A. and Vaughan, G.M. (4th edn) (2005) *Social Psychology,* Harlow: Pearson Prentice Hall.

Hollway, W., Cooper, T., Johnston, A. and Stevens, R. (2007) The psychology of sex and gender. In Cooper, T. and Roth, I. (eds) *Challenging Psychological Issues,* Milton Keynes: Open University Press.

Hollway, W., Lucey, H. and Phoenix, A. (2007) *Social Psychology Matters,* Milton Keynes: Open University Press.

Homans, G.C. (1961) *Social Behaviour: Its Elementary Forms,* New York: Harcourt, Brace and World.

Huston, T.L., Surra, C., Fitzgerald, N.M. and Cate, R.M. (1981) From courtship to marriage: mate selection as an interpersonal process. In Langdridge, D. and Taylor, S. (2007) *Critical Readings in Social Psychology,* Milton Keynes: Open University Press.

Iemmola, F. and Ciani, A. (2009) New evidence of genetic factors influencing sexual orientation in men: Female fecundity increase in the maternal line. *Archives of Sexual Behaviour,* 38(3): 393–9.

Impett, E., Beals, K. and Peplau, L. (2003) Testing the investment model of relationship commitment and stability in a longitudinal study of married couples. In Nathaniel, J. (ed.) *Love, Romance, Sexual Interaction: Research Perspectives from Current Psychology*, New Brunswick, NJ: Transaction Publishers.

Ingoldsby, B.B. (1995) Mate selection and marriage. In Goodwin, R. (1999) *Personal Relationships Across Cultures*, London: Routledge.

Iwao, S. (1993) *The Japanese Woman: Traditional Image and Changing Reality*. Cambridge, MA: Harvard University Press.

Jacobson, J. and Willie, D. (1986) The influence of attachment pattern on developmental changes in peer interaction from the toddler to the pre-school period. In Durkin, K. (1995) *Developmental Social Psychology*, Oxford: Blackwell.

Jerstad, S. (2005) An examination of why people remain in violent dating relationships: A comparison between the investment model and attachment theory. *Dissertation Abstracts International; Section B, The Sciences and Engineering*, 65: 4834.

Johnson, M. (1998) Love and Entrapment: Wife beating in America. In Goodwin, R. (1999) *Personal Relationships Across Cultures*. London: Routledge.

Joinson, A.N. (2001) Self disclosure in computer-mediated communication: the role of self awareness and visual anonymity. In Brace, N. and Westcott, H. (2002) *Applying Psychology*, Milton Keynes: Open University Press.

Joinson, A. and Littleton, K. (2002) Computer mediated communication: living, learning and working with computers. In Brace, N. and Westcott, H. (2002) *Applying Psychology*, Milton Keynes: Open University Press.

Kandel, D.B. (1978) Similarity in real-life adolescent friendship pairs. *Journal of Personality and Social Psychology*, 36: 306–12.

Karney, B.R. and Bradbury, T.N. (1995) Assessing longitudinal change in marriage : An introduction to the analysis of growth curves. *Journal of Marriage and the Family*, 57: 1091–1108.

Karney, B.R. and Bradbury, T.N. (1997) Mapping the human heart (and mind). *PsychCritiques*, 24(7).

Kenrick, D.T. and Keefe, R.C. (1992) Age preferences in mates reflect sex differences in human reproductive strategies. In Barrett, L., Dunbar, R. and Lycett, J. (2002) *Human Evolutionary Psychology*, Basingstoke: Palgrave Macmillan.

Kenrick, D.T., Keefe, R.C., Bryan, A., Barr, A. and Brown, S. (1995) Age preferences and mate choice among homosexuals and heterosexuals: A case for modular psychological mechanisms. *Journal of Personality and Social Psychology*, 69: 1166–72.

Kerckhoff, A.C. and Davis, K.E. (1962) Value consensus and need complementarity in mate selection. *American Sociological Review*, 27: 295–303.

Kerns, K.A. (1994) A longitudinal examination of links between mother–child attachment and children's friendships in early childhood. *Journal of Social and Personal Relationships*, 11: 379–81.

Kiecolt-Glaser, J.K. Fisher, L., Ogrocki, P., Stout, J.C., Speicher, C.E. and Glaser, R. (1987) Marital disruption, marital disruption, and immune functioning. *Psychosomatic Medicine*, 49: 31–4.

Kiecolt-Glaser, J.K., Malarkey, W.B., Chee, M., Newton, T., Cacioppo, J.T., Mao, H. and Glaser, R. (1993) Negative behaviour during marital conflict is associated with immunological down-regulation. *Psychosomatic Medicine*, 55: 395–409.

Kiecolt-Glaser, J.K. and Newton, T.L. (2001) Marriage and Health: His and Hers. *Psychological Bulletin*, 127(4): 472–503.

Kiecolt-Glaser, J.K., McGuire, L., Robles, T. and Glaser, R. (2002) Psychoneuroimmunology: Psychological influences on immune functioning and health. *Journal of Consulting and Clinical Psychology*, 70(3): 537–47.

Kiecolt-Glaser, J.K., Preacher, K.J., MacCallum, R.C., Atkinson, C., Malarkey, W.B. and Glaser, R. (2003) Chronic stress and age-related increases in the proinflammatory cytokine IL-6. *Proceedings of the National Academy of Sciences of the United States of America*, 100: 9090–5.

Kinsey, A.C., Pomeroy, W.B. and Martin, C.E. (1948) *Sexual Behaviour in the Human Male*, Philadelphia: Saunders.

Kinsey, A.C., Pomeroy, W.B. and Martin, C.E. (1953) *Sexual Behaviour in the Human Female*, Philadelphia: Saunders.

Kitzinger, C. and Coyle, A. (1995) Lesbian and gay couples: Speaking of difference. *The Psychologist*, 8(2). Special issue: Personal Relationships. pp. 64–9.

Kitzinger, C., Coyle, A., Wilkinson, S. and Milton, M. (1998) Towards a lesbian and gay psychology. *The Psychologist*, November 1998.

Klein, M. (1926) The psychological principles of early analysis. In Cooper, T. and Roth, I. (2007) *Challenging Psychological Issues*, Milton Keynes: Open University Press.

Kobak, R.R., Cole, H.E., Ferenz-Gillies, R., Fleming, W.S. and Gamble, W. (1993) Attachment and emotional regulation during mother-teen problem solving: A control theory analysis. *Child Development*, 64: 231–45.

Kobak, R. and Hazan, C. (1991) Attachment in marriage: The effects of security and accuracy of working models. *Journal of Personality and Social Psychology*, 60: 861–9.

Kraut, R., Mukhopadhyay, T., Szczypula, J., Kiesler, S. and Scherlis, B. (2000) Information and communication: alternative uses of the internet in households. In Brace, N. and Westcott, H. (2002) *Applying Psychology*, Milton Keynes: Open University Press.

Kroeber, A.L. and Kluckhohn, L. (1952) Culture: A critical review of concepts and definitions. In Hogg, M.A. and Vaughan, G.M. (4th edn) (2005) *Social Psychology*, Harlow: Pearson Prentice Hall.

Kulik, J.A., Mahler, H.I.M. and Moore, P.J. (1996) Social comparison and affiliation under threat. *Journal of Personality and Social Psychology*, 71: 967–79.

Kurdek, L.A. (1992) Relationship stability and relationship satisfaction in cohabiting gay and lesbian couples: A prospective longitudinal test of the contextual and interdependence models. *Journal of Social and Personal Relationships*, 9(1): 125–42.

Kurdek, L.A. (1995) Developmental changes in relationship quality in gay and lesbian cohabiting couples. *Developmental Psychology*, 31(1): 86–94.

Kurdek, L.A (2004) Are gay and lesbian cohabiting couples really different from hetero sexual married couples? *Journal of Marriage and Family*, 66: 880–901.

Kurdek, L.A. (2005) What do we know about gay and lesbian couples? *Current Directions on Psychological Science*, 14(5).

Kurdek, L.A. (2006) The nature and correlates of deterrents to leaving a relationship. *Personal Relationships*, 13.

Langlois, J.H., Kalakanis, L., Rubenstein, A.J., Larson, A., Hallam, M. and Smoot, M. (2000) Maxims or myths of beauty: A meta analytic and theoretical review. *Psychological Bulletin*, 126: 390–423.

Larson, R.W. (1990) The solitary side of life: An examination of the time people spend alone from childhood to old age. In Miell, D. and

Dallos, R. (1996) *Social Interaction and Personal Relationships*, Milton Keynes: Open University Press.

Lawson, H. and Leck, K. (2006) Dynamics of internet dating. *Social Science Computer Review*, 24(2): 189–208.

Le, B. and Agnew, C.R. (2003) Commitment and its theorized determinants: A meta analysis of the investment model. *Personal Relationships*, 10(1): 37–57.

Lee, L. (1984) Sequences in separation: A framework for investigating endings of personal (romantic) relationships. In Duck, S.W. (1984) *Personal Relationships 4*, London and New York: Academic Press.

Levy, M.B. and Davis, K.E. (1988) Love styles and attachment style compared: their relations to each other and to various relationship characteristics. *Journal of Social and Personal Relationships*, 5(4): 439–71.

Lieberman (1977) cited in Durkin, K. (1995) *Developmental Social Psychology*. Oxford: Blackwell.

Liu, J.H., Campbell, S.M. and Condie, H. (1995) Ethnocentrism in dating preferences for an American sample: The In-group bias in social context. In Hogg, M.A. and Vaughan, G.M. (4th edn) (2005) *Social Psychology*, Harlow: Pearson Prentice Hall.

Lorenz, K.Z. (1935) The companion in the bird's world. *Auk*, 54: 245–73.

Lucey, H. (2007) Families. In Hollway, W., Lucey, H. and Phoenix, A. *Social Psychology Matters*, Milton Keynes: Open University Press.

Lycett, J. and Dunbar, R. (2000) Mobile phones as lekking devices among human males. *Human Nature*, 11(1).

Lyons-Ruth, K., Alpern, L. and Repacholi, B. (1993) Disorganized infant attachment classification and maternal psychosocial problems as predictors of hostile-aggressive behavior in the preschool classroom. *Child Development*, 64: 572–85.

McLanahan, S.S. and Bumpass, L. (1988) Intergenerational consequences of family disruption. *American Journal of Sociology*, 94: 130–52.

Mackey, R.A., Diemer, M.A. and O' Brien, B.A. (2004) Relational factors in understanding satisfaction in the lasting relationships of same sex and heterosexual couples. *Journal of Homosexuality*, 47(1): 111–36.

Main, M., Kaplan, N. and Cassidy, J. (1985) Security in infancy, childhood and adulthood: a move to the level of representation. *Monographs of the Society for Research in Child Development*, 50: 66–104.

Main, M. and Solomon, J. (1990) Procedures for identifying infants as disorganized/disoriented during the Ainsworth Strange Situation. In Greenberg, M., Cicchetti, D. and Cummings, E.M. (eds) *Attachment in the preschool years: Theory, research and intervention* (pp. 121–60), Chicago: University of Chicago Press.

Manzoor, S. (2009) Jayasree Sen Gupta wanted to get married, *The Guardian*, 24 August.

Mastekaasa, A. (1995) Age variations in the suicide rates and self reported subjective well being of married and never married persons. *Journal of Community and Applied Social Psychology*, 5: 21–39.

McKenry, P.C.V. and Price, S.J. (1995) Divorce: A comparative perspective. In Goodwin, R. (1999) *Personal Relationships Across Cultures*, London: Routledge.

McKillip, J. and Riedel, S.L. (1983) External validity of matching on physical attractiveness for same and opposite sex couples. *Journal of Applied Social Psychology*, 13: 328–37.

Mickelson, K.D., Kessler, R.C and Shaver, P.R (1997) Adult attachment in a nationally representative sample. *Journal of Personality and Social Psychology*, 73(5): 1092–106.

Miell, D. and Croghan, R. Examining the wider context of social relationships. In Miell, D. and Dallos, R. (1996) *Social Interaction and Personal Relationships*, Milton Keynes: Open University Press.

Miell, D. and Dallos, R. (1996) *Social Interaction and Personal Relationships*, Milton Keynes: Open University Press.

Miller, J.B. and Hoicowitz, T. (2004) Attachment contexts of adolescent friendships and romance. *Journal of Adolescence*, 27(2): 191–206.

Moghaddam, K.M., Taylor, D.M. and Wright, S.C. (1993) *Social Psychology in Cross Cultural Perspective*, New York: W H Freeman.

Moller, N., McCarthy, C. and Fouladi, R. (2002) Earned Attachment Security: Its relationship to coping resources and stress symptoms among college students following relationship break ups. *Journal of College Student Development*, 43(2): 213–30.

Montoya, M., Horton, R. and Kirchner, S. (2008) Is actual similarity necessary for attraction? A meta analysis of actual and perceived similarity. *Journal of Social and Personal Relationships*, 25(6): 889–922.

Moore, C.W. (1997) Models of attachment, relationships with parents and sexual behaviour in at-risk adolescents. *Dissertation Abstracts International: Section B The Sciences and Engineering*, 58: 3322.

Morrison, V. and Bennett, P. (2006) *An Introduction to Health Psychology*, Pearson.

Murstein, B.I. (1972) Physical attractiveness and marital choice. In Gross, R.D. (1993, 3rd edn) *Psychology: The Science of Mind and Behaviour*, Bath: Hodder and Stoughton.

Mwamwenda, T.S. and Monyooe, L.A. (1997) Status of bride wealth in an African culture. In Goodwin, R. (1999) *Personal Relationships Across Cultures*, London: Routledge.

Myers, J., Madathil, J. and Tingle, L. (2005) Marriage satisfaction and wellness in India and the United States: A preliminary comparison of arranged marriages and marriages of choice. *Journal of Counseling and Development*, 83: 183–90.

Moller, N.P., McCarthy, C. and Fouladi, R.T. (2002) Earned attachment security: Its relationship to coping resources and stress symptoms among college students following relationship break up. *Journal of College Student Development*, 43(2): 213–30.

Mott, F.L. and Moore, S.F. (1979) The causes of marital disruption among young American women: An interdisciplinery perspective. *Journal of Marriage and the Family*, 41: 335–65.

Ogden, J. (2007) *Health psychology*, McGraw Hill/Open University Press.

ONS (2005) http://www.statistics.gov.uk/STATBASE/ssdataset. asp?vlnk=9126

ONS (2009) http://www.statistics.gov.uk/hub/population/families/ marriages--cohabitations--civil-partnerships-and-divorces/index. html

Pamporov, A. (2007) Sold like a donkey? Bride-price among the Bulgarian Roma. *Journal of the Royal Anthropological Institute*, 13: 471–6.

Parke, R.D., MacDonald, K.B., Beitel, A. and Bhavnagri, N. (1988) The role of the family in the development of peer relationships. In K. Durkin (1995) *Developmental Social Psychology*. Oxford: Blackwell.

Pawlowski, B. and Dunbar, R.I.M. (1999) Impact of market value on human mate choice decisions. In Barrett, L., Dunbar, R. and Lycett, J. (2002) *Human Evolutionary Psychology*, Basingstoke: Palgrave Macmillan.

Pawlowski, B. and Dunbar, R.I.M. (2001) Human mate choice decisions. In Barrett, L., Dunbar, R. and Lycett, J. (2002) *Human Evolutionary Psychology*, Basingstoke: Palgrave Macmillan.

Pawlowski, B., Dunbar, R. and Lipowitz, A. (2000) Tall men have more reproductive success. In Barrett, L., Dunbar, R. and Lycett, J. (2002) *Human Evolutionary Psychology*, Basingstoke: Palgrave Macmillan.

Pawlowski, B and Sorokowski, P (2008) Adaptive preferences for leg length in a potential partner. *Evolution and Human Behaviour*, 29(2): 86–91.

Payne, S. and Walker, P. (1996) *Psychology for Nurses and the Caring Professions*, Buckingham: Open University Press.

Pittman, F. (1989) *Private Lies: Infidelity and the Betrayal of Intimacy*, New York: Norton.

Prigerson, H.G., Maciejewski, P.K. and Rosenheck, R.A. (1999) The effects of marital dissolution and marital quality on health and health service use among women. In Kiecolt-Glaser, J.K. and Newton, T.L. (2001) Marriage and Health: His and Hers. *Psychological Bulletin*, 127(4): 472–503.

Qureshi, R.B. (1991) Marriage strategies among Muslims from south Asia. In Zaida, A. and Shuraydi, M. (2002) Perceptions of arranged marriages by young Pakistani Muslim women living in a western society, *Journal of Comparative Family Studies*, 33(4): 495–514.

Randall, S. (1995) Low fertility in a pastoral population: Constraints or choice? In Barrett, L., Dunbar, R. and Lycett, J. (2002) *Human Evolutionary Psychology*, Basingstoke: Palgrave Macmillan.

Reis, H.T. and Franks, P. (1994) The role of intimacy and social support in health outcomes. In Smith, E. and Mackie, D. (2000) *Social Psychology*. Hove: Psychology Press.

Rhatigan, D. and Axsom, D.K. (2006) Using the investment model to understand battered women's commitment to abusive relationships. *Journal of Family Violence*, 21: 153–62.

Rollie, S. and Duck, S. (2006) Divorce and dissolution of romantic relationships: Stage models and their limitations. In Fine, Mark, A. (ed.) *Handbook of Divorce and Relationships Dissolution*, Mahwah, NJ: Lawrence Erlbaum Associates Publishers.

Ross, C.E., Mirowsky, J. and Goldsteen, K. (1990) The impact of the family on health: The decade in review. In Kiecolt-Glaser, J.K. and Newton, T.L. (2001) Marriage and Health: His and Hers. *Psychological Bulletin*, 127(4): 472–503.

Rusbult, C.E. (1983) A longitudinal test of the investment model. The development (and deterioration) of satisfaction and commitment in heterosexual involvement. *Journal of Personality and Social Psychology,* 45: 101–17.

Rusbult, C.E., Verette, J., Whitney, G.A., Slovik, L.F. and Lipkus, I. (1991) Accommodation processes in close relationships: Theory and preliminary empirical evidence, *Journal of Personality and Social Psychology,* 60: 533–78.

Rusbult, V. and Van Lange, P.A.M. (1996) Interdependence processes. In Higgins, E.T. and Kruglanski, A. (eds) *Social Psychology: Handbook of Basic Principles,* New York: Guilford Press.

Rusbult, C. and Zembrodt, I.M. (1983) Responses to dissatisfaction in romantic involvements: A multi dimensional scaling analysis. *Journal of Experimental Social Psychology,* 19: 274–93.

Russell, A. and Finnie, V. (1990) Pre-school children's social status and maternal instructions to assist group entry. *Developmental Psychology,* 26: 603–11.

Rutter, M., Quinton, D. and Hill, J. (1990) Adult outcomes of institution-reared children: males and females compared. In Cooper, T. and Roth, I. (2007) *Challenging Psychological Issues,* Milton Keynes: Open University Press.

Sbarra, D.A. and Nietert, P.J. (2009) Divorce and death: Forty years of the Charleston Heart Study. *Psychological Science,* 20(1): 107–13.

Sears-Roberts Alterovitz, S. and Mendelsohn, G. (2009) Partner preferences across the lifespan: online dating by older adults. *Psychology and Ageing,* 24(2).

Sedikides, C., Oliver, M. and Campbell, W. (1994) Perceived benefits and costs of romantic relationships for women and men: Implications for exchange theory. *Personal Relationships,* 1: 5–21.

Selfhout, M., Denissen, J., Branje, S. and Meeus, W. (2009) In the eye of the beholder: Perceived, actual and peer-rated similarity in personality, communication and friendship intensity during the acquaintance process. *Journal of Personality and Social Psychology,* 96(6): 1152–65.

Shackelford, Todd K. (1998) Divorce as a consequence of spousal infidelity. *Romantic Love and Sexual Behavior: Perspectives from the Social Sciences.* de Munck, Victor C. pp. 135–53, Westport, CT: Praeger Publishers/Greenwood Publishing Group.

Shulman, S., Scharf, M., Lumer, D. and Maurer, O. (2001) Parental divorce and young adult children's romantic relationships: Resolution of the divorce experience. *American Journal of Orthopsychiatry,* 71(4): 473–8.

Siegel, J. M. (1990) Stressful life events and use of physician services among the elderly: The moderating role of pet ownership. *Journal of Personality and Social Psychology, 58*: 1081–6.

Silverman, I. (1971) Physical attractiveness, *Sexual Behaviour,* 22–25 September.

Simon, R.W., Eder, D. and Evans, C. (1992) The development of feeling norms underlying romantic love among adolescent females. *Social Psychology Quarterly,* 55(1): 29–46.

Simpson, J.A., Rholes, W.S. and Nelligan, J.S. (1992) Support seeking and support giving within coupes in an anxiety-provoking situation: The role of attachment styles. *Journal of Personality and Social Psychology,* 63: 434–46.

Simpson, J.A., Rholes, W.S. and Phillips, D. (1996) Conflict in close relationships: An attachment perspective. *Journal of Personality and Social Psychology,* 71(5): 899–914.

Simpson, J.A., Winterheld, H., Rholes, W.S. and Orina, M. (2007) Working models of attachment and reactions to different forms of caregiving from romantic partners. *Journal of Personality and Social Psychology,* 93(3): 466–77.

Singh, D. (1993) Adaptive significance of female physical attractiveness: role of waist to hip ratio. In Barrett, L., Dunbar, R. and Lycett, J. (2002) *Human Evolutionary Psychology*, Basingstoke: Palgrave Macmillan.

Singh, D. and Luis, S. (1995) Ethnic and gender consensus for the effect of waist to hip ratio on judgement of women's attractiveness. In Barrett, L., Dunbar, R. and Lycett, J. (2002) *Human Evolutionary Psychology*, Basingstoke: Palgrave Macmillan.

Singh, R. and Ho, S.Y. (2000) Attitudes and attraction: A new test of the attraction, repulsion, and similarity dissimilarity asymmetry hypotheses. *British Journal of Social Psychology*, 39(2): 197–211.

Slavin, S. (2009) Instinctively, I'm not just a sexual beast: The complexity of intimacy among Australian gay men. *Sexualities,* 12(1): 79–96.

Smith, E. and Mackie, D. (2000) *Social Psychology*, Hove: Psychology Press.

Snyder, M., Berscheid, E. and Glick, P. (1985) Focusing on the exterior and the interior: Two investigations of the initiation of personal relationships. In Smith, E. and Mackie, D. (2000) *Social Psychology*, Hove: Psychology Press.

Sprecher, S. (1998) Insiders perspectives on reasons for attraction to a close other. *Social Psychology Quarterly,* 61(4): 287–300.

Sprecher, S. (1998) Social exchange theories and sexuality. *Journal of Sexual Research,* 35(1): 32–43.

Society Matters (2009) Issue 12. http://www.open.ac.uk/ socialsciences/__assets/l3qzxw7ixnli7kr5s4.pdf.

Sprecher, S. and Chandak, R. (1992) Attitudes about arranged marriages and dating among men and women from India. In Goodwin, R. (1999) *Personal Relationships Across Cultures,* London: Routledge.

Srinivasan, P. and Lee, G. (2004) The Dowry system in Northern India: Women's attitudes and social change. *Journal of Marriage and Family,* 66(5): 1108–1.

Sroufe, L.A. and Fleeson, J. (1986) Attachment and the construction of relationships. In Durkin, K. (1995) *Developmental Social Psychology,* Oxford: Blackwell.

Stack, S. (1990) The impact of divorce on suicide: New micro level data. *Journal of Marriage and Family,* 52: 119–27.

Stringer, C. and McKie, R. (1996) African exodus: The origins of modern humanity. In Barrett, L., Dunbar, R. and Lycett, J. (2002) *Human Evolutionary Psychology,* Basingstoke: Palgrave Macmillan.

Terling- Watt, T. (2001) Explaining divorce: An examination of the relationships between marital characteristics and divorce. *Journal of Divorce,* 35(3–4): 125–45.

Thibaut, J.W. and Kelley, H.H. (1959) *The Social Psychology of Groups,* New York: Wiley.

Tooby, J. and Cosmides, L. (1992) The psychological foundations of culture. In Miell, D., Phoenix, A. and Thomas, K. (3rd edn) (2007) *Mapping Psychology Book 1,* Milton Keynes: Open University Press.

Tran, S. and Simpson, J.A. (2009) Prorelationship maintenance behaviours: The joint roles of attachment and commitment. *Journal of Personality and Social Psychology,* 97(4): 685–98.

Traupmann, J., Petersen, R., Utne, M. and Hatfield, E. (1981) Measuring equity in Intimate Relationships. In Van Yperen, N. and Buunk, B. (1990) A longitudinal study of equity and satisfaction in intimate relationships. *European Journal of Social Psychology,* 20: 287–309.

Triandis, H., Lambert, W., Berry, J., Lonner, W., Heron, A., Brislin, R. and Draguns, J. (eds) (1980) *Handbook of Cross Cultural Psychology,* Boston: Allyn and Bacon.

Trivers, R.L. (1972) Parental investment and sexual selection. In Barrett, L., Dunbar, R. and Lycett, J. (2002) *Human Evolutionary Psychology*, Basingstoke: Palgrave Macmillan.

Umadevi, L., Venkataramaiah, P. and Srinivasulu, R. (1992) A comparative study on the concept of marriage by professional and non-professional degree students. *Indian Journal of Behaviour*, 16(6): 27–33.

Van Yperen, N. and Buunk, B. (1990) A longitudinal study of equity and satisfaction in intimate relationships. *European Journal of Social Psychology*, 20: 287–309.

Wallerstein, J.S. and Lewis, J. (1998) The long-term impact of divorce on children: A first report from a 25 year study. In Shulman, S., Scharf, M., Lumer, D. and Maurer, O. (2001) Parental divorce and young adult children's romantic relationships: Resolution of the divorce experience. *American Journal of Orthopsychiatry*, 71(4): 473–47.

Veitch, R. and Griffith, W. (1976) Good news, bad news: affective and interpersonal effects. *Journal of Applied Social Psychology*, 6: 69–75.

Walster, E., Walster, G.W. and Berscheid, E. (1978) *Equity Theory and Research*. Boston, MA: Allyn.

Walther, J.B. (1996) Computer mediated communication: impersonal, interpersonal and hyper personal interaction. In Brace, N. and Westcott, H. (2002) *Applying Psychology*, Milton Keynes, Open University Press.

Walster, E., Aronson, V., Abrahams, D. and Rottman, L. (1966) Importance of physical attractiveness in dating behaviour. *Journal of Personality and Social Psychology*, 4: 508–16.

Waters, E., Wippman, J. and Sroufe, L.A. (1979) Attachment, positive affect and competence in the peer group: two studies in construct validation. In Durkin, K. (1995) *Developmental Social Psychology*, Oxford: Blackwell.

Waynforth, D. (2001) Mate choice trade-offs and women's preference for physically attractive men. *Human Nature*, 12(3): 207–19.

Waynforth, D. and Dunbar, R. (1995) Conditional mate choice strategies in humans: evidence form lonely hearts advertisements. *Behaviour*, 132: 735–79.

Waynforth, D., Delwadia, S. and Camm, M. (2005) The influence of women's mating strategies on preference for masculine facial architecture. *Evolution and Human Behaviour*, 26(5): 409–16.

Wei, M., Russell, D.W., Mallinckrodt, B. and Vogel, D.L. (2007) The experiences in Close Relationship Scale (ECR)-Short Form: Reliability, validity, and factor structure. *Journal of Personality Assessment*, 88: 187–204.

Whitty, M. (2008) Revealing the 'real' me, searching for the 'actual' you: Presentations of self on an internet dating site. *Computers in Human Behaviour*, 24(4): 1707–23.

Whyte, M.K. (1990) Dating, mating and marriage. In Goodwin, R (1999) *Personal Relationships Across Cultures*. London: Routledge.

Williams, A. and Merten, M.J. (2009) Adolescents online social networking following the death of a peer. *Journal of Adolescent Research*, 24(1): 67–90.

Wienke, C. and Hill, G.K. (2009) Does the 'marriage benefit' extends to partners in gay and lesbian relationships? Evidence from a random sample of sexually active adults. *Journal of Family Issues*, 30(2): 259–89.

Wood, C., Littleton, K. and Oates, J. (2002) Lifespan development. In Cooper, T. and Roth, I. (eds) (2007) *Challenging Psychological Issues*, Milton Keynes: Open University Press.

Wood, L.J., Gilesw-Corti, B., Bulsara, M. and Bosch, D.A. (2007) More than a furry companion: The ripple effect of companion animals on neighbourhood interactions and on sense of community. *Society and Animals*, 15: 43–56.

Xioahe, X. and Whyte, M.K. (1990) Love matches and arranged marriages: A Chinese Replication. *Journal of Marriage and Family*, 52: 709–22.

Yelsma, M. and Athappilly, K. (1988) Marriage satisfaction and communication practices: Comparisons amongst Indian and American couples. *Journal of Comparative Family Studies*, 19: 37–54.

Zaida, A. and Shuraydi, M. (2002) Perceptions of arranged marriages by young Pakistani Muslim women living in a western society. *Journal of Comparative Family Studies*, 33(4): 495–514.

Zimmerman, P., Becker-Stoll, F., Grossman, K., Scheurer-Englisch, H. and Wartner, U. (2000) Longitudinal attachment development from infancy through adolescence. *Psychologie in Erziehung und Unterricht*, 47(2): 99–117.

Index

Entries in **bold** refer to glossary definitions

A

Acculturation, 133
Acculturative stress, 133, **162**
Adult attachment interview, 8–9, 50–1, **162**
Ainsworth, M. 7, 44–6
Arranged marriages, formation
  and dating websites, 134–5
  in modernising cultures, 131–2
  in traditional cultures, 129–31
  in western cultures, 132–3
  young women's perceptions of, 134
Arranged marriages, maintenance
  and breakdown
  regulation of, 136–40
  satisfaction and happiness in, 137–9
  conflict in, 139
  breakdown of, 140–2
Argyle, M. 1, 5, 85
Attachment theory, 40–6 *see also*
  Bowlby, J.
  continuity hypothesis, 40, 43 52–8,
    108
  evolutionary basis of attachment, 42
  internal working models, 40, 43,
    52, 108
  psychodynamic basis of
    attachment, 43
Attachment styles
  adult attachment interview, 8–9,
    50–1, **162**
  dimensions of, 48–50
  in the Love Quiz, 46–8
  in the strange situation, 44–6
Attachment styles and later
  relationships
  in adolescent relationships, 55–6
  in adult relationships, 46–51, 56–8
  in children's friendships, 53–5
  dealing with conflict, 92–4
  parental divorce, 108
  relationship breakdown, 56–7

B

Benefits of relationships *see* Effects of
  relationships
Bowlby, J. 7, 40, 41–3, 52
Breakdown of relationships, 100 –13
  see also Conflict and
  Communication
  equity in, 87
  gender differences, 104

infidelity, 110–12
  of long-term relationships, 104–6
  of short-term relationships, 102
  parental divorce, 107
  predisposing factors, 106–7
Buss, D., 6, 7, 19, 28, 29, 33–6, 126
Byrne, D., 3, 64–5

C

Collectivist cultures
  and equity, 87
  and formation of relationships 128
  in Hofstede's model, 124–5,
  and mate preferences, 126,
Communication patterns
  and attachment style, 82, 92–4
  gender differences, 92
  Gottman's study of, 113–14
  mediated relationships, 17, 69
  negative patterns of, 94–5, 112–13
  relationship satisfaction, 95
  same-sex relationships, 15, 97
Conflict
  arranged marriages and, 133, 139
  attachment styles and, 82, 92–4
  causes of, 91
  dealing with, 91–2
  effects on physical health, 9–10,
    151–3
  same-sex couples, 16, 97
Content analysis, 26–7, 71, **163**
Continuity hypothesis, **163** *see also*
  Attachment theory
Crisis in social psychology, 10–18
Critical social psychology, 11–12
Cross-cultural challenges to
  mainstream psychology, 13–14
Cross-cultural studies
  in evolutionary psychology, 6
  of body shape preferences, 6–7
  of chastity, 36
  of physical attractiveness, 64

Cultural variations in relationships,
  see Arranged marriages
Culture, **164**
  definitions of, 122–3
  models of cultural variation, 123–4
Cunningham, M.R., 24, 25

D

Darwin, C.
  evolution by natural and sexual
    selection, 21–2
  inter-sexual selection, 22
  intra-sexual selection, 22
Data types
  physiological/material data, 9–10,
    145
  qualitative data, 12, 133–4
  self-report data, 145, 149
  statistical data, 145
Developmental social psychology, 7–9
Discursive social psychology, 11–13,
  164
Dissolution of relationships
  barriers to dissolution, 105, **163**
  Duck's phase model, 116–19
  Gottman's two factor model, 113
  Lee's model, 118–19
Duck, S. 85, 102, 106, 116–18
Dunbar, R. 21, 22, 23, 25, 26, 38, 64

E

Economic theories of relationship
  regulation, **164** *see also under*
  Equity theory, Interdependence
  theory and Social exchange theory
Effects of relationships, 143–60
  life expectancy, 146, 150, 155, 158
  mental health and well-being,
    147–50, 154–5
  physical health 146–7
  self-esteem, 154
  marriage benefit, 156

Environment of evolutionary
adaptation, 21, **164**
Epidemiology, 9, **164**
Epidemiological studies
of mental health, 147–9
of physical health, 146–7
Equity
definition, 4
measuring, 87–8
objective and subjective, 86
role in relationship breakdown, 104
Equity theory, **164**
assumptions of, 85–8
cultural criticisms of, 13
evidence for, 86–7
Ethical issues, 4 28, 30, 111
Evolutionary social psychology, 5 –7,
165
Experimental social psychology, 3–5,
66, **165**

F, G
Filter model of attraction, 60, 74–6,
78, 103
Goodwin, R., 13–14, 125, 128, 129–
30
Gottman, J., 5, 94–5, 113

H, I
Health psychology, 9–10, **165**
Hofstede, G., 123–4
Hogg, M., 3, 5, 13
Homosexual relationships *see* Same-
sex relationships
Human reproductive behaviours *see*
Sexual selection
Interdependence
in the developing relationship, 78
in same-sex couples, 16
types of, 79
Interdependence theory, **166**
assumptions of, 88–9

evidence for, 89–90
investments, 88
Internal working model, **166** *see also*
Attachment theory
Interpersonal attraction, 60–9, **166**
attraction, 61
contact, 62
physical appearance, 62–4
similarity, 64–5, 66–7
Investments, **166** *see also*
Interdependence theory

K, L
Kiecolt–Glaser, J., 9–10, 152, 147,
151, 152, 153, 155, 159
Kurdek, L.A., 16, 68, 82, 96, 115
Lee, L., 118–19
Love Quiz, 46–8

M
Maintenance of relationships, 81–95
definition of, 82
economic theories of, 81–95
processes in, 91
conflict and communication in,
91–5
Matching hypothesis, 60, 73–4, 78
Mate preferences, **166**
and personal column adverts,
25–6
in cross-cultural studies, 126–8
Mediated relationships
formation of, 69–71
social support in, 159
types of, 17

P, Q, R
Parental investment theory, **167**
assumptions of, 30–2
evaluation of, 32–3
Personal column adverts, 25–7, 64,
67, 68, 134–5

Pawlowski, B., 23, 25, 26
Predisposing factors, 167 *see also*
  Breakdown of relationships
Qualitative research
  study of girls talking, 12–13
  qualitative data, 109–10
  perceptions of arranged
    marriages, 133–4
Questionnaires, 36–7
Reproductive success, 25, 31–3,
  34–5, **168**
Reward/need satisfaction theory,
  76–7, 78, **168**
Rusbult, C., 77, 88–90, 91, 96

S

Same-sex relationships
  barriers to ending, 105
  breakdown of, 114–15
  challenges of studying, 14–17, 98
  formation of, 68–9
  marriage benefit, 150
  mate preferences, 68
  regulation, 96–8
  social support, 97
Satisfaction in long-term
  relationships, 95–6, 137–8
Schmitt, D.P., 19
Self-esteem, 44, 76, 84, 103
Sexual selection
  inter-sexual selection, 21,
  intra-sexual selection, 22
  and physical attraction, 23–5, 154
  and mate preferences, 25–27
  and human reproductive
    behaviours, 28–30

Sexual strategies theory, 19, **168**
  assumptions of, 33–4
  evaluation of, 35–6
Simpson, J., 57, 58, 93
Singh, D., 24, 65, 126,
Social exchange theory, **168**
  comparison level, 83
  comparison level for alternatives,
    84
  economic assumptions of, 82–4
  evaluation of, 84–5
  in experimental social psychology,
    3
  minimax principle, 84
Social support
  in arranged marriages, 138
  definition of, 157
  gender differences in, 158–9
  online relationships, 157
  pets, 160
  protection hypothesis, 156
  recovery from illness, 155
  same-sex relationships, 97
  support networks, 157–8
Sociobiological explanations *see under*
  Sexual strategies theory and
  Parental investment theory
Strange situation, **168** *see also*
  Attachment styles

T, V, W
Trivers, R., 19, 30–3
Vaughan, G., 3, 5, 13
Waynforth, D., 24, 25, 64

Reading guide

This table identifies where in the book you'll find relevant information for those of you studying or teaching A-level. You should also, of course, refer to the Index and the Glossary, but navigating a book for a particular set of items can be awkward and we found this table a useful tool when editing the book and so include it here for your convenience.

Topic	AQA	WJEC	Page
Adolescent experiences and adult relationships	x		52–6
Attraction and formation		x	24, 61
Benefits of relationships: buffering from stress		x	146–56
Benefits of relationships: self-esteem		x	154
Breakdown of relationships	x	x	100–13
Childhood experiences and adult relationships	x		7
Duck's phase model		x	116–18
Human reproductve behaviour	x		28–30
Interaction with peers	x		53–5
Lee's model		x	118–19
Parent–child relationships	x		44–50
Parental investment	x		30–33
Relationships in different cultures	x		122–4, 129, 34

Topic	AQA	WJEC	Page
Reward/need satisfaction theory	x		76–7
Sexual selection	x		21–30, 154
Social exchange theory	x	x	82–4
Sociobiological explanations of formation		x	19, 30-3
Understudied relationships: homosexual		x	14–17, 68–9, 98, 105, 114–15, 150
Understudied relationships: mediated		x	17, 69–71, 159